Better Thinking for Better Results

Better
THINKING
For
Better
RESULTS

Cathy Lasher

Better Thinking for Better Results

First published in 2015 by
Panoma Press Ltd
48 St Vincent Drive, St Albans, Herts, AL1 5SJ UK
info@panomapress.com
www.panomapress.com

Cover design by Michael Inns
Artwork by Karen Gladwell

ISBN 978-1-909623-87-3

This book is available online and in all good bookstores.

Contents

Acknowledgements

Many people have helped me with this book. You know who you are – and I thank you hugely. You have variously inspired me, supported me, informed me, and made me seemingly endless cups of tea. I credit you only with what is good in this book, and take full responsibility myself for any errors.

I also want to acknowledge here that I have included in the book many stories to help explain and illustrate key points. These stories come from the experiences of a number of clients with whom I have worked over the years. I thank you for generously and courageously sharing your stories with me, and hope that I have disguised the details enough to honour the confidentiality agreements we have had, without diverting from the truth of the experiences.

Introduction

*"It is not enough to have a good mind.
The main thing is to use it well."*

– René Descartes

Get better results through focused thinking

You have limited time and a demanding life. You are already good at a lot of what you do. You live in an uncertain world. You may be wondering if this is 'as good as it gets'. You have a sense that you could be doing things *better*, but don't quite know what to do to make that happen.

You know that it is important to be thoughtful about what you are doing, and you may know that some kind of 'reflective thinking' would be a good idea, but you have no real idea how to do that.

This book is a practical toolkit. It will show you something really powerful – how to achieve more through the power of focused thinking. It will teach you the specific tools you need to focus your thinking, so that you can elicit maximum benefit from investing time in focused, reflective thinking.

I have many executive coaching clients who tell me that even when they are able to snatch some time from their incredibly hectic lives to think and reflect, they don't always know how to use that time most effectively. As one senior executive put it, "I know I should spend time reflecting. But when I do, I often just end up cycling round and round the same points. It seems like rather a waste of time!"

Other clients have a similar refrain, acknowledging a sense they have that they should be doing 'something', but aren't sure quite what that 'something' is. When pushed, they say that perhaps what they need is some sort of personal or non-technical professional development to help them do things better, more easily, more efficiently, more effectively.

If these laments sound familiar to you, this book is just what you need.

A practical toolkit

You might think of this book as a self-coaching toolkit. Many of my executive coaching clients also say that one of the most valuable things about having a coach is creating the time to think about things – and here is the really important part – with someone to help them structure their thinking. This book can do that for you.

This book is a practical toolkit for a structured way of reflecting. (Reflecting is a fancy name for a particular kind of focused thinking.) I have developed a simple model – EDGE-it – that is a map for reflective, focused thinking. This map is easy to learn, and powerful to apply.

In addition to the basic EDGE-it map, the book includes a number of clearly signposted practical components to help you get the most from your reading and from working with the material: questions, exercises, tools, case studies and examples. These are here to prompt some thinking on your part, and will help you clarify thoughts you already have.

Key to symbols:

 Tool

 Exercise

 Case Study/Example

Three 'time zones'

You can use the EDGE-it map in three different 'time zones'.

You can use it in the traditional reflecting time zone – **looking back** on events that have already happened. The purpose of that sort of reflection is primarily to extract valuable learning from previous experiences, to make sure things go even better next time. That's important, and I want to help you improve your skills in doing that.

You can also use the EDGE-it map **'in the moment'**. This is a speeded up version of the looking back reflection, what can be called 'thinking on your feet' – using today's buzzword, 'mindfulness' – to enhance your thinking, and improve your performance and results.

Finally, you can extend the practical application of these techniques to a **future orientation,** helping you set and achieve goals in the context of an uncertain future.

Why I have written this book

In recent years, in my work as a coach and trainer, working over literally thousands of hours with senior and mid-level executives from a wide range of organisations, it has become clear to me that reflective thinking isn't really well embedded into the organisational world. As a psychotherapist, the concept of reflective practice is extremely familiar to me. For the past couple of years I have been teaching a degree-level course in Reflective Therapeutic Practice to both trainee and established psychotherapists. It is extraordinary how much professional and personal development has resulted for the students of those courses. When I looked for resources to use with my corporate clients, too, clients like you who are wrestling with the demands of leadership and with the complex and important challenges of personal and professional development, there was a complete dearth of materials. I have written this book to begin to fill that gap. Why shouldn't our corporate leaders – you! – have access to the same quality thinking tools that our psychotherapists and counsellors have?

Map of the book

The book is divided into four main sections:

 ☼ The first sets out the case for reflective thinking, and helps you assess your own attitudes towards, and skills in, reflecting.

☼ The second section provides the practical 'map', introducing EDGE-it, which can be used to support your reflective practice.

☼ The third section is a guide to application. It includes a workbook – tools and techniques combined with opportunities to practise your reflective thinking on issues that are important to you – on things that have already happened, or in-the-moment situations, or on goals you want to achieve.

☼ Finally, the book concludes with a section on reflective practice as a key leadership skill and suggestions for how you can take these skills even further, and leverage the very reflective skills you will have developed, for even more powerful outcomes.

How to use this book

You can take time working your way through this book, stopping on the practical elements as you come across them, answering questions, working through exercises, practising with the tools. Or you can read through the book and come back to the practical elements at a later time that suits you. Or you can dip in and out of the book, whatever suits your personal style and 'time budget'.

Whilst it will likely be most powerful and beneficial to undertake the process in full, even a taste of the process will help you learn something that will help you make improvements. Whichever approach you take, please do answer the questions, do the exercises, practise using the tools. They are not just for reading about, they are for doing!

Final word from the soapbox

I am passionate about the value of reflective thinking. I have seen first-hand how many people's work and overall quality of life have been improved by doing the type of reflective thinking that is explained and illustrated in this book. In the pages that follow I am going to share with you the EDGE-it map that works in your sort of organisational context, that works in the three different time zones, together with many other practical tools and techniques that make it possible for you to incorporate the practice of reflective thinking into your everyday life, helping you to achieve better results through focused thinking.

So if you are ready, let's get started.

PART I

The Case for Reflective Thinking

"By three methods we may learn wisdom: First, by reflection, which is noblest; second, by imitation, which is easiest; and third, by experience, which is the bitterest."

– Confucius

Better Thinking for Better Results

CHAPTER ONE

Reflective Practice Can Help You

Can it really?

In a word – yes!

You have probably already come across the concept of reflective practice in some context or other. You certainly know that thinking about what you are doing is a good idea. You have known that since you were a small child, and a parent or teacher encouraged you to think while you were taking an exam, or preparing to begin a project. It may have been that as part of a sports activity you engaged in post-event reviews, possibly watching film of your performance and analysing that.

What kind of thinking, though? That's the problem really. Someone asked me the other day: "What is the most compelling business reason you can give me to encourage me to engage in reflective practice?" Perhaps you have the same question. Here is what I said:

"You already know you should be doing this. It makes
sense to spend time thinking about the important things
in your life, both at home and at work. The problem is
that until now no one has told you how to do it."

That is what this book is for.

What is reflective practice?

There are many definitions, most of which centre on thinking about an experience with the specific purpose of learning from it. The originator of the term was Donald Alan Schön (1930–1997), an American academic. Schön's formal training was as a philosopher, but he is most remembered for his interest in reflective practice and learning systems. Schön first coined the phrase 'Reflective Practice' in 1983 in his book *The Reflective Practitioner*. Many of the concepts had been around for some time by the time he published his book, and numerous people have added to the body of knowledge around reflective practice in the three decades since Schön's seminal book was published. (See Appendix 1 for a brief history of Reflective Practice, together with a number of models that have been developed to support the practice.)

Until now, this term has primarily been applied in teaching and in the health professions, including counselling and psychotherapy. It is time that those in the commercial world are able to benefit from the powerful practice of reflection, purposefully applied to the specific challenges in that context.

Recent published research ('*Reflection on Work Improves Job Performance,*' Harvard Business School Working Knowledge – May 2014 Research & Ideas, by Giada Di Stefano et al.) demonstrated that as little as 10 minutes of reflection brought significant improvements in learning and performance. Their conclusion was that the automatic, unconscious process of 'learning by doing', when combined with a controlled, conscious attempt at 'learning by thinking' yielded more effective learning, and therefore enhanced performance. Why would your experience be any different?

It is a well-known definition of insanity to keep doing the same thing, expecting a different result. You are already doing what you can to improve your performance, and yet there are still things you could be doing better. How are you going to make the improvements you want to make if you keep doing things the same way?

Using exercises

I am acutely conscious that some of the exercises in the book may seem very basic to you. You may well wonder why I am asking you to write down your thoughts for some of these, especially those that do seem quite basic. This is not because I want to create a schooldays workbook! Rather it is because the process of organising our thoughts into words and sentences, as well as the process of actually writing, engages more parts of our brains in the thinking and reflecting activity. This means that the thinking is more thorough and more robust – and ultimately more useable.

For the rest of this chapter I am going to explore the benefits of reflective practice with you. I also invite you to experiment with it by engaging in a number of exercises. These exercises work on at least two levels. On the most obvious level, they are prompts to help you think about and make explicit some of what is going on for you, the context from which you are considering establishing reflective practice as part of your everyday life. And they have another benefit as well: they help you begin to *do* some focused thinking, including taking things through to being made explicit. They are designed to engage many of your reflective functions, including thinking, feeling, sensing, and visualising.

So, can reflective practice help *you*?

If you want to engage with the exercises in this book as you go along, this is your first opportunity. (It is also fine to carry on reading, and come back to any of the activities at a later time.)

List here what you hope for from reading this book. At this point it doesn't matter how realistic your hopes are, so feel free to write down whatever you want:

I hope this book can help me:

_____

_____

_____

_____

_____

_____

_____

_____

_____

Maybe you think you are too busy to read this book because you are under so much pressure.

Part of that pressure may come from the amount of time you spend doing the 'wrong' things. These can be things that turn out to be unnecessary, or that need to be re-done. Or things that lead to unwanted outcomes that could have been anticipated if you had just stopped and thought a bit better. By the way, it *is* necessary to stop – at least for a moment – if you want to think better. It is physiologically impossible to change your thinking without at least a brief press of the 'pause' button.

Spectrum of Reflectivity

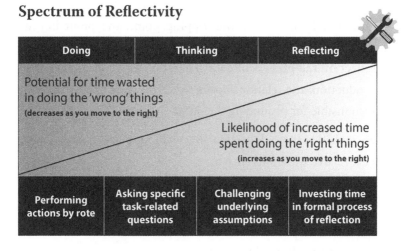

Doing	Thinking	Reflecting
Potential for time wasted in doing the 'wrong' things (decreases as you move to the right)	Likelihood of increased time spent doing the 'right' things (increases as you move to the right)	
Performing actions by rote	Asking specific task-related questions	Challenging underlying assumptions	Investing time in formal process of reflection

The objective is to move from the left to the right in this spectrum, which requires that you stop for a moment and think. This diagram illustrates that as you move to the right side of the spectrum, increasing the likelihood of spending time doing the 'right' things, the pressure of 'doing' can be relieved. I am going to show you how to do that, how to move from simply doing, through asking specific task-related questions, through the process of challenging underlying assumptions, to investing time in effective reflective practice.

EXAMPLE:

A client I will call John, a managing director in a major merchant bank, was the head of a team that was responsible for producing a certain daily report. This was a constant source of irritation for his team – and for John – as it was often difficult to obtain the data for inclusion in the report on a timely basis due to failures in technology. Sometimes literally hours could be spent chasing the data. It often seemed to be necessary for John to intervene with the IT department to get the data produced. One day, John crossed the 'tipping point', the point beyond which he could no longer tolerate this situation, and paused to reflect on the process of data generation and collection, report production, and relationships between his team and the IT team responsible for producing the data.

He looked at the task itself in all its various steps, asking himself task-related questions such as:

Who is responsible for producing the data?

What holds up the overall production of data?

What do I need to know about the collection and analysis of this data?

What aspects of this process are the most difficult?

Who needs this information?

When do they need it by?

He then questioned some of the underlying assumptions:

Do the recipients of the report use all the aspects of the report?

How else could they get the information?

What alternatives are there to my team producing a report?

Are we really the best team to be producing this report?

Is this report really the best way to circulate the analysed data?

Is 'daily' the best frequency?

Finally, John reflected on the situation, asking himself:

With the broadest possible perspective on this situation, what is the best way forward?

Taking everything into account, using all the creative thinking I can muster, what options shall we consider?

Eventually, after going through this reflective process, John concluded that much of the system around the report should be restructured, giving end users real time access to a specific portion of the data, and that other data should continue to be analysed by his team and distributed on a weekly basis. He also realised that some of the key people in the IT team did not understand the significance of the data, which meant that they did not understand the significance of delaying the distribution of that data, and he undertook a short training session with those people.

Investing time – even a very little time – will help you make positive changes to the way you are doing things, and bring benefits. You have picked up the book, so maybe there is already part of you that is ready to commit to at least dipping your toe into reflective activity.

You undoubtedly want to excel and stand out in your work environment.

Precisely how do people excel in your context? Your organisation will have measures of excellence. These may be made known to you through a competence framework, either formally or informally. They are likely to form part of your personal objectives for the year, or feature in your development planning.

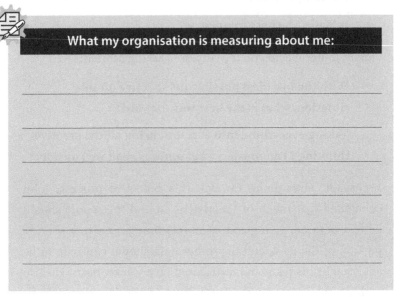

What my organisation is measuring about me:

Think about the effort you are making to achieve strong results in these areas. Doesn't it make sense to understand exactly what is required, how your specific contributions can be enhanced, and how they will be measured? If you could leverage all your skills to the nth degree, wouldn't you be foolish not to?

Take a moment now to think about those aspects of your performance that are being measured. What *don't* you know about these aspects that would be useful to you to know? How could you find out?

CHAPTER 1 - Reflective Practice Can Help You

A competence that is often measured in leaders in organisations is the skill of promoting equal opportunities and diversity. This is typically one of the criteria under the broad heading of 'people management'. Perhaps this is one of the measurements used in your organisation?

But what does it mean?

One competence framework I have seen goes on to explain:

Sharing and promoting best practice

Communicating and modelling appropriate standards of behaviour

Challenging intolerance and discriminatory behaviour where they arise

Promoting the value of diversity

Then I ask again, but what does it mean?

Do you know what your organisation's policy is on diversity and equal opportunity? Have you seen such a policy written down?

(Perhaps *you* are responsible for this policy!) How would you translate the words into meaning, and from there into specific actions? And how would those actions best be measured?

It would be easy to imagine how not clarifying the measure of excellence could easily result in much wasted effort. If you want to excel in your commercial environment, a necessary starting position is to know how such excellence is measured. This ensures that the actions you take are moving you towards those measures of excellence.

You are likely to have little niggles which are getting harder to ignore.

There is a concept in psychotherapy that is called 'edge of awareness'. This term describes something which is just on the periphery of your awareness, something that when you are finally able to see it or articulate it, you think yes, that's been there for some time, but which isn't clear to you at this precise moment.

Those little niggles you experience are something similar. These niggles are the slight discomforts you have – and generally dismiss – about your health, or your relationship, or a business challenge. For a while, a niggle is easy enough to dismiss. And eventually it gets bigger, and clearer, and you know that you have to do something about it. How useful would it be to spot this earlier, to bring forward that moment when you say, "I *knew* it! I just knew this was going on!"?

This kind of thing often provides the content for a coaching session. A client will come in and say, "I have a problem with something, and I really should have picked it up sooner." As we explore the issue, it often transpires that there was a time when, in retrospect, the client saw the signals that this issue was emerging. The key is to be able to spot the signals earlier.

Let me give you an example. Sylvia, an HR professional in a large financial services firm, came to a recent coaching session saying that her board had withdrawn the authorisation they had previously granted her to establish a new programme for emerging leaders. She was hugely disappointed, and believed that this was a poor decision on the part of the board. She did acknowledge, however, her strongly held belief that the time for influencing their decision had passed, and that she would need to work with the new, restricted budget. Through reflecting on the events leading up to the withdrawal of authorisation, Sylvia realised:

> For the last month, as a result of several severe operating pressures, she had neglected to maintain close relationships with several of her key stakeholders, neglecting the relationships generally, and the flow of communication about her plans specifically.

☼ At the previous month's board meeting questions had been raised about the business case for the new programme. Sylvia thought she'd dealt with the challenges well, but on reflection acknowledged that perhaps a more rigorous evaluation would have revealed some dissatisfaction among key board members.

Taking time out on a regular basis to do a broad perspective review – outside the blinkered focus often so much a part of working to deadlines in a fast-paced environment – can pinpoint areas of niggly discomfort. These areas can then be addressed in a timely fashion, preventing the sort of undermining event that Sylvia unfortunately experienced.

Don't wait for your niggles to reach a crucial, make-or-break point. Take the time to spot the key signals earlier and then take the time to reflect on them and take appropriate action. This is an opportunity to take the corrective action needed to enable you to spend time doing the *right* things.

You think you are not at your best, but cannot quite pinpoint the problem.

There is a personal resource audit that you can do to help begin to make these things clearer to you. This is a tool you can use to focus on what you have available to you in terms of your own resources. It is also helpful to use in weighing up options in the service of decision making. In every case, deficits need to be compensated for in order to avoid problems.

There are four domains of resource available to you:

Domain:	Includes:	At your most replete, you are:
Physical	• Energy • Coordination • Nutrition • Health • Fitness • Strength • Physical environment	Well-nourished, fit, and strong enough to do what needs to be done in surroundings that support you
Emotional	• Self-awareness • Resilience • Motivation • Interpersonal sensitivity • Influence • Intuitiveness • Conscientiousness	In rapport with self and others, feeling motivated and resilient
Spiritual	• Flexibility • Centred-ness • Integrity • Values-led • Self responsible • Responsive • Curious • Breadth of vision • Connection	Aware of a sense of purpose and meaning in your life
Intellectual	• Literate • Numerate • Understanding • Reasoning • Decision-making • Abstract concepts • Analysis • Problem solving	Able to understand quickly, reason and make the world coherent

Four Resource Domains

Rate yourself in each of these domains, using a scale from 0–10, where 0 is entirely impoverished, and 10 is fully replete. Then consider:

Where I am most fit? *(This is where you feel more resource-full, with reserves to fall back on)*

_____

_____

_____

_____

_____

Where am I least fit? *(This is where you feel resource-less and undernourished)*

_____

_____

_____

_____

_____

_____

It is often the case that a shortfall in one aspect in a domain can be compensated for by extra resources in another in the same domain, and indeed that a shortfall in one domain can be compensated for by extra resource in another, at least in the short term. For example, when you are very tired (physical), it may be that making sure you eat well, or are in supportive physical surroundings can compensate (also physical). Or when you are under a good deal of pressure because of difficulties in an important relationship (emotional), relying on your sense of purpose (spiritual) can help you.

From completing the above resource audit, where do you have niggles that might need to be attended to?

My niggles at the moment include:	
Niggle	**Domain**

You are working to leverage your efforts to maximise outcomes in your organisation.

Recent trends mean that you have to do more, with fewer resources, in less time, and to a higher standard. This means that leveraging all of your resources is absolutely essential – and that includes you and your time. You are being asked to tackle a wide variety of business success indicators, including increasing sales, margins, and/or profits, improving staff retention, managing more difficult supplier relationships, dealing with more demanding and better-educated customers, just to name a few.

Reflective practice can help you find the ways to do this.

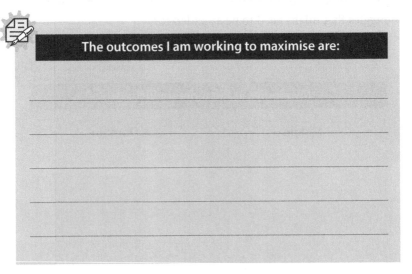

The outcomes I am working to maximise are:

These are likely to be quite high-level objectives. Take some time to deepen your thinking. Even just a few minutes will help. Challenge yourself to write down three additional thoughts about each of the outcomes you just articulated. Use the prompt questions to help you:

☼ **What aspect of this is likely to give me a quick win?**

☼ **What is the next step to take in that direction?**

☼ **What do I feel in relation to taking that next step?**

It may be that these three trigger questions provoke additional thoughts for you. If they do, either make some brief notes now and diarise a time to come back to them, or take a break from reading and devote some time now to these additional thoughts.

_____

_____

_____

_____

_____

_____

Perhaps you want to create more balance in your life without taking your foot off the career pedal.

Sometimes you feel that things are out of proportion in your life. You spend 'too much' time on some aspects, 'not enough' in others. You want more balance in your life. You recognise the importance of making time for family and friends, and recreational activities. But you are working in a highly competitive environment. To succeed, you feel you have to keep pushing, working harder and harder, and smarter and smarter.

Using reflective practice can help you gain clarity about your priorities, helping you to identify how much time and effort you want to put into the various aspects of your life. One very useful tool to use in connection with this is a sectioned wheel.

Sectioned Wheel

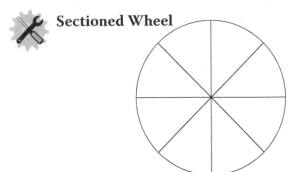

A sectioned wheel can be used for many things. Start by identifying an overall area to think about, and drawing a wheel, creating a number of sections in the wheel. I recommend eight. Each wedge is then labelled with one of the aspects of the area you want to think about. Once you have done that, you consider your level of satisfaction with each of the aspects.

Let's work though an example of how a sectioned wheel can be used.

Roger's Story

Roger, a 40-something regional director in an international business consultancy, with a new wife and two teenage stepchildren, was feeling very pressured and was seriously considering leaving his much-loved job to take on work that would be much less demanding. On reflection, he created the following wheel, labelling the wedges to indicate areas of his life that were important to him. The overall area was 'quality of my current life'. He chose the following eight aspects to explore further: current job, personal and professional development, new marriage, old marriage, relationship with stepchildren, friends, financial position, and health and fitness.

Then, seeing the centre of the wheel as 0 and the outer edge as 10, Roger ranked his current level of satisfaction with each life area as it was at the time of constructing this wheel by drawing a line to create a new outer edge. For Roger, the rankings were as follows:

Aspects	Level of satisfaction
Current job	?
Personal and professional development	3
New marriage	?
Old marriage	7
Relationship with step-children	4
Friends	8
Financial position	10
Health and fitness	8

He then drew new 'perimeters' in each of the relevant wedges, creating a circle that looked like this:

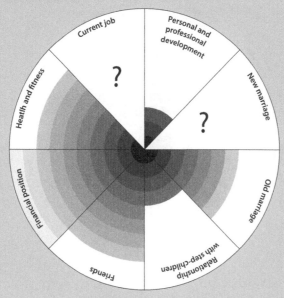

After following these steps and thinking about his levels of satisfaction, Roger realised that he was unable to rate his level of satisfaction easily in two of the wedges: with work and with his new marriage. He recognised that despite apparently feeling generally very satisfied with both, there was a 'danger zone' for him, related to the interplay of pressures from work with pressures from his new marriage and stepchildren. He therefore created another wheel to help him focus on and evaluate the various pressures from both of those sources.

This second wheel took these two wedges from the first wheel into a new eight-section wheel, looking at both topics in more detail.

Roger's second wheel included sections he labelled: spending regular time with his new family, travel requirements of current job, working hours, remuneration, promotion possibilities, communications with key work stakeholders, communications with new wife, and professional development.

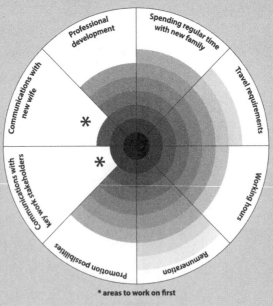

* areas to work on first

Aspects	Level of satisfaction
Spending regular time with new family	7
Travel requirements of current job	8
Working hours	7
Remuneration	9
Promotion possibilities	7
Communications with key work stakeholders	2
Communications with new wife	3
Professional development	6

From this, Roger was able to identify that the key areas to work on were his communciations with both his new wife and his key stakeholders at work. From his focused thinking on this, he identified that he had a familiar route of making unilateral decisions, a route which had been creating some problems for him. Once he realised this, he was able to define some different communication strategies for use both with his new wife and with his key stakeholders at work.

Now create your own wheel. Look at the sectioned wheel below. Label the wedges with the words that are most meaningful for you. One possible format includes the following eight: Career, Money, Health, Friends and Family, Significant Other/ Romance, Personal Growth, Fun and Recreation, and Physical Environment.

Feel free to use any or all of these, and/or any others that would be more meaningful for you. There is no magic to having exactly eight wedges. You could divide the wheel into more sections, or even leave out one or two.

Then, seeing the centre of the wheel as 0 and the outer edge as 10, rank your current level of satisfaction with each life area *as it is at the moment* by drawing a line to create a new outer edge.

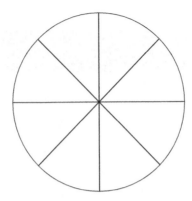

Now have a look at the shape of the circle. The new perimeter of the circle represents *your* 'wheel of life', at least the way in which you think about it at this time. What strikes you about this? What would you need to focus on to create more balance?

There are other things in your life that are important to you that you don't make time for.

You probably have a number of things that you say you want to do – exercise perhaps, or spending more time with your children, or delegating more. You value your health, your relationships at home and at work, and yet somehow they often slip to the bottom of the pile. These are things that you say are important, and yet somehow you don't find the time to do them. You may even have (annoying) people in your life who say things to you like,

"If you really wanted to do it, you would find the time (or the way)." Take a minute now to think about the kind of things *you* say are important, and that you still don't do, and write them in the box below.

There is a psychological dynamic called a 'competing commitment'. This means that in addition to the commitment you have to do one thing (exercise more, spend more time with your children, delegate more), you have another, *hidden*, commitment that conflicts with it. This hidden commitment is based on certain assumptions that may or may not be true. The following worksheet is adapted from Robert Kegan & Lisa Lahey's *Immunity to Change*, Harvard Business School Publishing, (2009).

Stated improvement goal	What is actually happening instead - implying competition with the stated improvement goal	Worry that is embedded in succeeding at the stated improvement goal	Hidden commitment revealed by the worry	Big assumption underpinning the hidden commitment (and this is key)
I want to...	What is happening instead	I am afraid that if I achieve my stated improvement goal...	This worry implies that...	It seems that I assume that...

Competing Commitments Worksheet

I want to...	What is happening instead	I am afraid that if I achieve my stated improvement goal...	This worry implies that...	It seems that I assume that...
I want to delegate more to my team	I still keep more of the tasks (especially the good ones) instead of delegating them	If I delegate more, I will overload my team members, which will make me look like an insensitive manager	I also want to be seen as sensitive to other people	If I delegate more to my busy team they will think I don't care about them and stop working so well for me

Now try your own example. Kegan and Lahey say that if you don't feel you are 'screwed' when you get to the final column, you haven't done it right! They describe it as driving with your foot on the brake and the accelerator at the same time.

I want to...	What is happening instead	I am afraid that if I achieve my stated improvement goal...	This worry implies that...	It seems that I assume that...

Once you have completed the table, take some time to think about the underlying big assumptions in the final column. Are they true? What evidence do you have? What contradictory evidence do you have? How could you test these assumptions further?

_____

_____

_____

_____

_____

You are willing to develop a new behaviour.

As noted above, it is a well-known definition of insanity to keep doing the same thing and to expect a different result. You are already doing what you can to improve your performance, and yet there are still things you could be doing better. How are you going to make the improvements you want to make if you keep doing things the same way?

Developing a new behaviour requires concentration and concerted effort. We could think of this new behaviour as a good habit – and good habits can pay off. Think about a time when you made the effort to acquire a new behaviour. Perhaps you started a new exercise programme, or obtained a new phone, or started work in a new team. You might want to identify more than one, and then see if there are any common threads.

Habit or behaviour	Difficulties in acquiring the new habit or behaviour	Benefits of the new habit or behaviour	How long it took	Factors that helped make the new habit possible

What common threads are there?

_____

_____

_____

_____

_____

Stuart completed this exercise. He discovered that for him the common thread was putting time for the new habit into the diary.

Rosemary completed the exercise. She discovered that for her the common thread was committing to the new habit out loud to another person.

Lucy also completed the exercise. For her, the common thread was focusing on and fully exploring the benefits of adopting the new habit.

Roy's common thread was getting back to plan after 'failing' to employ the new habit, rather than immediately giving up.

Acquiring this new habit, the habit of reflective practice, can help you. All you need to do is give it a try. Try this process for 30 days – really try it – and I guarantee you that you will see improvements.

I hope that you have taken the opportunity to do some of the reflections in this chapter. (Thinking about the questions posed is reflecting, and whether or not you wrote down your answers to the questions, the thinking in and of itself was the start of a reflective process.) Perhaps some things have emerged from this reflective activity.

- **You may be clearer about the pressures you are under**
- **You may want to gain more clarity about what it is your organisation wants from you**
- **You may know more about the various conflicts you are feeling and what resources you have available to support you**
- **You may understand more about how you acquire new habits**

What *has* emerged for you? Make a note on the next page of any insights you have gained from this first chapter. Remember that the very process of organising your thoughts into words and sentences and writing them down helps to make them more useable.

So, if you are ready to give it a try, turn to the next chapter and I will show you how investing a bit of time – sometimes just seconds – can get you much improved outcomes and save you significant time in the long run.

KEY POINTS

Reflective practice is a way of focusing your thinking.
✿
Forcing yourself to articulate your thoughts explicitly can make them clearer and more useful.
✿
There is an apparent paradox in that spending time doing focused thinking will actually save you time. This is because spending time doing focused thinking will help you spend more time doing the 'right' things.
✿
Clarifying what aspects of your performance are being evaluated can help you take the right actions to improve your performance against those key measures.
✿
Ignored niggles only get bigger and work against you.
✿
You can sabotage your hard work towards effecting change as a result of hidden 'competing commitments'. It is possible to work out what they are so that future efforts aren't wasted.
✿
You can learn new habits. The habit of reflective practice could usefully be one of them.
✿
Your own points from this chapter:

_____

_____

_____

_____

_____

KEY TOOLS
INTRODUCED IN THIS CHAPTER

Spectrum of Reflectivity

✿

Four Resource Domains

✿

Sectioned Wheel

✿

Competing Commitments Worksheet

CHAPTER TWO

Invest a Bit of Time to Reap Significant Benefits

"We cannot solve our problems with the same thinking we used when we created them."

– Albert Einstein

Are you naturally reflective?

It goes without saying that people are different. Some will tend more naturally to reflection than others. So before you begin to acquire this new practice, it will be helpful to think about your natural style. Don't worry, even if reflection doesn't come naturally to you, you can still learn how to do it and how to benefit from it.

The theory of learning styles as developed by David Kolb (originally published in his book *Experiential Learning: Experience As The Source Of Learning And Development,* 1984) and as extended by Peter Honey and Alan Mumford while they were working on a project for the Chloride corporation in the 1970s, suggests that there are four main learning styles: Activist, Reflector, Theorist, and Pragmatist. They suggest that it is most beneficial to develop and be able to access all four styles. However, they acknowledge that most of us have a preferred style.

 ## Learning Styles Questionnaire

Here is a questionnaire based on Honey and Mumford's work that you can complete to determine your current learning style/communication preferences. The questionnaire is designed to find out your preferred learning/communication style(s). Over the years you have probably developed preferences, which this questionnaire will help you pinpoint. There is no right or wrong in terms of the final profile.

In order to get value from this, you should complete this honestly – think about how you *do* operate, not how you would like to. There is no time limit to this questionnaire.

If you agree more than you disagree with a statement put a tick by it ☑

- [ ] 1) 'Good enough' can never really be good enough unless you are aiming for mediocrity.
- [ ] 2) A focus on the here and now is more useful than a focus on the past or the future.
- [ ] 3) Achievement of goals is the thing I focus on most often.
- [ ] 4) An 'executive summary' is a valuable addition to any piece of work.
- [ ] 5) Asking questions is a good way to understand what someone is saying.
- [ ] 6) Being trusted with responsibility makes it easier to take on tasks I otherwise don't like much.

☐ 7) Disagreements are best resolved by rational dialogue.

☐ 8) Focus on the task, people!

☐ 9) I am a private person.

☐ 10) I am always looking for the best way to get something done.

☐ 11) I am happy to get my sleeves up and my hands dirty to help get the job done.

☐ 12) I am hugely encouraged by the praise of others.

☐ 13) I am often late to scheduled activities.

☐ 14) I am often the one who provides the necessary facts and figures.

☐ 15) I am slow to anger.

☐ 16) I can be interested in reading about a subject even without an immediate need for the information.

☐ 17) I can be motivated to work with people I don't particularly like if they respect me.

☐ 18) I can see how to keep things organised, and that is important.

☐ 19) I can vary my pace somewhat when necessary, though I prefer to be able to take my time.

☐ 20) I do what I can to avoid being wrong.

☐ 21) I don't like it when others 'beat around the bush' in their communication.

☐ 22) I don't mind upsetting others a bit in the interests of getting the task done.

☐ 23) I don't particularly enjoy working alone.

☐ 24) I feel energised and excited when diving into something new.

☐ 25) I find ambiguity unsettling.

☐ 26) I generally find questionnaires like this feel like a waste of time.

☐ 27) I get impatient if the team moves away
from the task in hand.

☐ 28) I have a reputation for saying what needs to be said.

☐ 29) I have a tendency towards perfectionism.

☐ 30) I have been told I have an explosive temper.

☐ 31) I like conversation to be useful.

☐ 32) I like to be able to draw general conclusions
from specific circumstances.

☐ 33) I like to be admired for my sound judgement.

☐ 34) I like to get my thoughts in good order before
I start to speak.

☐ 35) I like to read about new ideas.

☐ 36) I like to talk about my objectives in some detail.

☐ 37) I look for patterns to help me make meaning
of new information.

☐ 38) I love getting new gadgets that do useful things.

☐ 39) I love it when I have lots of activities and tasks
on the go at the same time.

☐ 40) I much prefer to work without interruption, and
when I am interrupted it really sets me back.

☐ 41) I need to be doing something.

☐ 42) I often find myself the group leader, and when
I am not I can get bored.

☐ 43) I often say "Let's do it a different way."

☐ 44) I often wonder 'Why change it?'

☐ 45) I prefer formal language rather than casual.

☐ 46) I prefer to speak after I hear something of
what others think.

☐ 47) I produce large quantities of output.

☐ 48) I speak at a moderate pace.

☐ 49) I tend to speak very quickly.

☐ 50) If I consult an instruction manual it is only because I am stuck.

☐ 51) In a new group I take my time before engaging with others.

☐ 52) Inaccuracies in others' communications frustrate me.

☐ 53) Intuitive based decision making is usually wrong in my opinion.

☐ 54) It doesn't matter if it doesn't work first time – trying again is fine.

☐ 55) It is great when I am appreciated for the contribution I have made.

☐ 56) It is important to understand the assumptions and facts on which decisions are based.

☐ 57) Logic is superior to irrationality.

☐ 58) My strong moral compass influences my decisions.

☐ 59) Other people find my office messy, but I know where everything is.

☐ 60) Others are often too slow or too haphazard in planning the next steps.

☐ 61) Others tend to regard me as serious.

☐ 62) Rational, logical thinking leads to the best decision making.

☐ 63) Spending time on preparation is generally boring.

☐ 64) The best decisions result from staying objective.

☐ 65) The divide between right and wrong is usually very clear to me.

☐ 66) The end almost always justifies the means.

☐ 67) When faced with a new situation I prefer to have an opportunity to do some research.

☐ 68) When I am angry I can be quite aggressive if I don't work at controlling my response.

Scoring

Please circle below the question numbers of any questions you ticked ☑.

Then, simply add up the number of questions you have circled in each column to give you a total in each of the four columns, i.e. max of 17 circled numbers in each column.

Activist	Reflector	Theorist	Pragmatist
3	6	1	2
13	7	5	4
17	8	16	10
21	9	18	11
23	14	25	12
24	15	29	22
26	19	32	27
39	20	35	28
41	33	37	30
42	34	53	31
43	40	56	36
47	45	57	38
49	46	58	44
54	48	62	50
59	51	64	55
63	52	65	60
68	61	67	66
___	___	___	___
___	___	___	___

Having scored your questionnaire, you will now have four scores ranging from 0–17 for each of the columns: for Activist, Reflector, Theorist and Pragmatist.

So, what does this show? The larger the number of circled answers in a column, the stronger your preference is for that learning/communication style. Very simply, the different styles could be described as follows:

Activist – If this is your preference, you are someone who learns best by doing things. You like to jump in. You enjoy new situations, and are unlikely to resist change. A potential downside is that you may have a tendency to do the thing most immediately obvious, rather than spend time weighing up other possibilities. You may also have a tendency to go into situations without adequate preparation.

Reflector – If this is your preference, you are someone who learns best by thinking about things. You like to think things over, and are good at listening and assimilating information. A potential downside is that you may hold yourself back from direct participation. You may also procrastinate, primarily as a result of being slow to make up your mind.

Theorist – If this is your preference, you are someone who learns best by finding the conceptual underpinning. You like to think things through carefully, and value the logical and objective path. A potential downside is that you may have a low tolerance for uncertainty or ambiguity, making creative problem solving difficult. You may also be full of 'shoulds' and 'musts'.

Pragmatist – If this is your preference, you are someone who learns best by focusing on the practical benefits, and testing things out in practice. You like to keep things realistic. A potential downside is the tendency to reject anything without an immediate practical application. You may also have a tendency to take the first expedient solution to a problem, rather than think around it more fully.

I will show you more about this in Chapter 3. If you have a relatively strong preference for Reflector then I can show you how to refine the process to extract even more value from it. If you haven't, if your learning preference is for one or more of the other styles, I will show you how to develop your reflector muscles so that you, too, can benefit from this way of noticing and thinking.

 Don't take my word for it – use this Reflective Map in the following exercise and see what benefit you derive:

Think about a recent meeting you attended, or experience you had, that would benefit from additional reflection. It will be most helpful if this is something that took place within the last week.

Reflective Map – 3 Step Abbreviated Model

 Step 1:

Write down everything you can remember by way of describing the meeting/experience. These questions might help you get started:

- ☼ **Who was there?**
- ☼ **When was it?**
- ☼ **Where was it held?**
- ☼ **What was it about?**
- ☼ **What were the outcomes?**
- ☼ **How did I feel about it at the time?**
- ☼ **How do I feel about it now?**

Step 2:

Now let's deepen the reflection on the meeting/experience, and work out what you make of it. Again, here is a list of questions that might help you get started:

- ☼ **What went well?**
- ☼ **What didn't go as well as I'd have liked?**
- ☼ **What would I like to have done differently?**
- ☼ **How satisfied am I with the outcomes?**
- ☼ **What else affected the way I felt about the meeting/ experience, then or now?**

_____

_____

_____

_____

Step 3:

And finally, let's connect it to an action: What next? Split your thinking into two categories:

What is there from that meeting/experience that needs to be done now?	What did I learn from my experience of that situation that I want to use for future experience?

Here is an example that may help you:

What is there from that meeting/experience that needs to be done now?	What did I learn from my experience of that situation that I want to use for future experience?
e.g., I realise that we never really clarified how my task fits with the task John has responsibility for. I need to speak to John to clarify this.	e.g., I realise that having real clarity about desired outcomes keeps unhelpful emotions out of the discussion. In future, when I anticipate an emotional response, I want to remember to clarify desired outcomes as part of the agenda.

When you have finished doing that, consider what the benefit was of doing this reflection. How important was it to have the prompt questions, and a structure for recording your thoughts?

_____

_____

_____

_____

The process is eminently doable.

There are five aspects to reflective practice that help determine its success. The first of these is that **reflective practice is an active process.** This means that it requires you to do something intentionally. It isn't something that just happens, you have to **do** it. And doing it means following some sort of specific steps. We will come later to the specific steps I'm recommending.

Reflective practice starts with and goes beyond simply describing. A first step in reflective practice is to describe an experience. This experience could be something that has already happened, something that is happening now, or something that is going to happen in the future. However, while it is a necessary first step, the description by itself is not enough. You have to do something with the description.

Reflective practice both requires and results in a broadened perspective. This may sound like a bit of convoluted language – and it is true. Going beyond description, as above, means that the experience also needs to be analysed. In order to analyse a situation as fully as possible, you need to look at it from many different perspectives, hence the *requirement* for a broadened perspective. And once the analysis is done, new insights will emerge, giving the *result* of a broadened perspective.

The past, present and future are linked through reflective practice. Sometimes you will be using reflective practice to look at an experience that happened in the past. You will be reflecting in the present, and your objective will be to extract learning and define actions that will bring benefits in the future. Then the links are clear. This is the way reflective practice was originally introduced.

Sometimes you will be using reflective practice to look at something that is happening right now, in the present, or even something you are anticipating happening in the future. So it may be less immediately clear how the past is relevant. But of course, your past has influenced who you are today. The thoughts and beliefs you already have influence your behaviour as well as your way of thinking.

Finally, reflective practice is personal. Resorting to stating the completely obvious, *you* are the person reflecting. You use your own thoughts and feelings to notice aspects of the experience that are important to you. Your own values and beliefs and previous experiences help you determine what is important. Two people reflecting on what looks like the same experience will have a different reflective outcome, even though some similar points may emerge.

Make the most of investing your time

When you reflect just a little, you are likely to start with monitoring the things you do. When reflective practice becomes part of who you are, you are likely to use reflective practice regularly to improve the way you do things in many different parts of your life. The questionnaire below can be used to help you assess the level of reflectivity in your life at any given time, and help you aspire to a higher level of reflectivity by describing what that higher level might look like. The higher the number of the statement in the questionnaire, the higher your level of reflectivity at that time.

Statement	Date		
	Often	Sometimes	Rarely
1. I monitor my processes, practices and the outcomes from my work.			
2. I evaluate my own performance using best practice benchmarks.			
3. I reflect on my interactions with others.			
4. I share my reflections with others and use their feedback.			
5. I use reflection as a trusted process to solve problems.			
6. I use reflection to improve the way I work.			

Self-Reflectivity Assessment Tool

You can use this questionnaire to monitor your degree of reflectivity at any time. I would not expect the level to remain constant. It would be useful to map your responses over time, and then consider the significance of any changes you notice. Complete the questionnaire now, and then every day for two weeks. Notice and evaluate the pattern of your responses.

Statement	Monday			Tuesday			Wednesday			Thursday			Friday		
	Often	Sometimes	Rarely	Often	Sometimes	Rarely	Often	Sometimes	Rarely	Often	Sometimes	Rarely	Often	Sometimes	Rarely
1. I monitor my processes, practices and the outcomes from my work.															
2. I evaluate my own performance using best practice benchmarks.															
3. I reflect on my interactions with others.															
4. I share my reflections with others and use their feedback.															
5. I use reflection as a trusted process to solve problems.															
6. I use reflection to improve the way I work.															

What factors seem to influence the pattern of your responses? How do you feel about the result? What can you do about that?

_____

_____

_____

_____

_____

_____

_____

_____

_____

_____

_____

_____

Once you have done that, complete the questionnaire once a week for a month. Try to complete the questionnaire at the same time each week.

Statement	Week 1			Week 2			Week 3			Week 4		
	Often	Sometimes	Rarely	Often	Sometimes	Rarely	Often	Sometimes	Rarely	Often	Sometimes	Rarely
1. I monitor my processes, practices and the outcomes from my work.												
2. I evaluate my own performance using best practice benchmarks.												
3. I reflect on my interactions with others.												
4. I share my reflections with others and use their feedback.												
5. I use reflection as a trusted process to solve problems.												
6. I use reflection to improve the way I work.												

Again, notice and evaluate the pattern of your responses.

_____

_____

_____

_____

What factors seem to influence the pattern of your responses? How do you feel about the result? What can you do about that?

_____

_____

_____

_____

I can give you a map that will show you *how* to be reflective

Remember that I said that most writing on reflective practice tells you that you should do reflective practice, but doesn't tell you how. I am suggesting that you use a map.

- ☼ Maps are really helpful. They describe the place you are going, and help you get back on course if you get lost.
- ☼ Maps and templates save time, and allow you to study the territory more meaningfully. The map only has to be drawn once, and then can be used over and over again.

> Each time you need to go there, you can refer to the map and free your mind to think of other things beyond the directions to the destination.

> ☼ Maps and templates show you the territory. With one glance you can take in a large amount of information about the ground you are going to cover, keeping the relationships in a stable perspective even as you move through the territory.

I found this on a children's geography website and thought it apposite:

Suppose we want to find a buried treasure, and the only person who knows where the treasure is cannot travel with us. How will we find the treasure? The individual who knows where the treasure is could describe to us in great detail how to get to and find the treasure. This might work, but what happens if we forget an important part of the instructions? We would have to travel all the way back and have them repeat again the description of where the treasure is hidden. We could have them write the description down for us. That way, we will not forget it. Having these instructions in hand, we can easily refer back to them as needed. A list of written directions would be a more useful tool, but what would happen if we got lost? Once we were off course, the written directions would no longer be of any use to us. These instructions only specified how to find the treasure from one specific starting point, and not from our current lost position. A map solves both of these problems.

Drawing a detailed map of the area around the treasure would allow us to take something with us so that we don't forget. If we get lost, we simply determine where on the map we are, and then continue towards our destination.

(http://www.kidsgeo.com/geography-for-kids/0025-usefullness-of-maps.php, accessed 21/8/13)

If you use a map for reflection, you will notice things differently.

Remember that 'edge of awareness' concept I mentioned in Chapter 1? This is a concept that was borrowed from the psychotherapy world. This relates to bringing knowledge to the forefront, to where you can use it. It is a concept that will be familiar to you if you are familiar with 'coaching' as it is used in the workplace. Executive or business coaching has at the heart of its philosophy the concept that the person being coached holds many answers within them. They may not be fully aware of these answers at any given moment, but with some time and skilful interrogation (by their coach or by themselves), the answers will reveal themselves. This is different from sports coaching, where the coach often includes a significant amount of *training* in their interactions, rather than simply helping the other to benefit from what they already know.

Carol, the MD of a hospitality business, was struggling to implement a new marketing strategy. She had spent many hours reading books and articles on the subject, looking for answers, and had engaged in numerous conversations with others in which she asked for advice. None of that really unlocked a solution with which she was completely comfortable. In fact, it seemed to serve to undermine her confidence in her own ability to resolve the issues.

As a result of a coaching session, Carol then tried following a reflective map. The details of the map at this point are less important than the general concept. The map included asking and answering a number of trigger questions to open thinking. The main unlocking trigger question for Carol was: 'What are the main lessons you have learned previously about implementing

51

new strategy?' Because she had relevant, albeit not identical, previous experience on which to draw, outlining previously learned lessons gave her the answers she'd been looking for. She also had the added bonus of increased confidence in herself, as she realised she *did* actually know what to do.

Using *this* map

In order to use well the map I am going to share with you in Chapter 4, you need to notice things differently. What do I mean by that?

Well, what I mean is that you will notice things on at least three different levels: cognitively, affectively and somatically.

Prompts for Noticing

Let's take these one at a time.

The first is **cognitively**. This means using your rational, logical senses. I imagine that this is pretty familiar to you. It is generally how you notice things. If I ask you to describe where you are right now, what kinds of things would you say? Take a minute to jot down some of your describing words:

_____

_____

_____

_____

_____

This cognitive noticing may include, for example:

    Inside or outside

    Colours you see

    Any people or objects you can see

    The temperature

    The size

    Any sounds you are aware of

A second level of noticing is **affectively**. Affect is to do with feeling, emotional feeling. So here you would use emotional words such as

Happy	Sad	Indifferent	Afraid
Upset	Hurt	Positive	Alive
Open	Good	Loving	Strong
Angry	Depressed	Helpless	Hopeless
Indifferent	Bad	Excited	Lonely

This is by no means a complete list. Furthermore, each of these words will have many variations, and indeed the words may mean different things to different people. For our purposes, that doesn't matter.

If you want to notice your own affect right now, there are some questions that can help you.

How do you feel about where you are right now?

How do you feel about what you can see?

How do you feel about the temperature, the size, the colours?

How would you describe your general mood?

What conflicting feelings are you aware of?

Try to stick to affective words such as the ones that appeared in the list above or variations/refinements of them. Be particularly cautious about including *thoughts*. They will have been collected in the first part, the cognitive noticing. Once you have recorded your initial feeling response, see if you can expand the description. Ask yourself:

What *kind* of [good, for example] is that?

Repeat this for each of the affective words you have chosen, and see how much deeper you can go.

The third level of noticing is **somatically**. This means to notice what physical sensations you are experiencing. These may or may not be related to the specific experience, but until you have noticed them, you cannot hope to extract any meaning that *may* be there.

For example, you may have a terrible headache. If you focus on this, notice the somatic sensation of the headache, you may come to notice that you are tensing your neck and shoulders. Further noticing may reveal that you are also slightly holding your breath. You may ascribe some meaning to this on reflection. You could notice that you are feeling slightly anxious, or tense. What could that be about? You may feel under time pressure. What could that relate to? You might also know that you got hit on the head yesterday at the cricket match, and the headache is unrelated to your current experience.

Take a minute right now to notice what bodily sensations you have. Take a further moment to reflect on what possible meaning they may have.

Somatic sensation	Possible meaning

Stick with it a few more minutes. Allow yourself time to notice at least a little bit more.

So what do you do with the different ways of noticing?

Having a different way of noticing what is happening will give you a different understanding of what is happening. You will be gathering more information, broadening your perspective on the experience.

From this broadened perspective you will be able to generate a wider and better range of options, and you will gain more clarity about which option is preferred. Following the map to its edges will then ensure that things get done. Your thinking will move from useful to use-able.

Something is happening all the time. It is easy to be overwhelmed by or oblivious to what is actually happening, which results in our taking frequent, and often unhelpful, shortcuts. Take a look at the cycle below, which could represent an effective pathway from noticing to action:

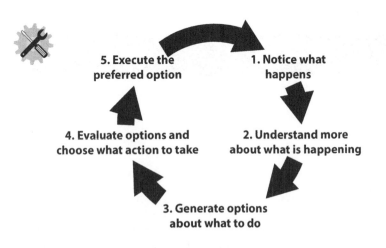

Reflective Map – 5 Step Extended Model

It is my impression from working with literally thousands of executives that many people spend merely seconds on step 1 – noticing what is happening – and then skip quickly to step 3 – generating options (though maybe only one) – and then rebound nearly immediately to step 5 – executing the preferred (or only) option. And the process stops there. There is generally no return to step 1, noticing what happens as a result of the option chosen. So much of the process is left out.

Following through on all the steps will greatly enhance your outcomes.

Maybe all this sounds too good to be true. Perhaps you are thinking it would be nice to believe that these benefits really are available, and perhaps you are thinking 'yes, but...'. Turn to the next chapter to see if I have anticipated your concern, and I hope I can convince you that adopting this reflective practice habit, using this reflective practice map, is absolutely worth a try.

KEY POINTS

There are four basic styles for learning
and communicating:

Activist

Reflector

Theorist

Pragmatist

These are based on work done by Kolb, and extended
by Honey and Mumford. Most people prefer one or two
of these styles more than the others.

✿

There are five key aspects to reflective practice:

It is active

It goes beyond description

It requires and results in a broadened perspective

It links the past, present and future

It is personal

✿

Without a deliberate methodology, most people tend
simply to go quickly from one experience to another.

✿

Noticing can be done at three levels: cognitively (in the
head, thinking), affectively (emotional feelings), and
somatically (felt, in the body).

✿

Using a reflective map can help you notice things
differently. This gives you a different understanding,
which helps you generate a wider and better range
of options. This helps you gain more clarity about
which option is preferable, and move from noticing to
powerful action.

Your own points from this chapter:

_____

_____

_____

_____

_____

KEY TOOLS
INTRODUCED IN THIS CHAPTER

Learning Styles Questionnaire

✿

Reflective Map –

3 step abbreviated model

5 step extended model

✿

Self-Reflectivity Assessment

✿

Prompts for Noticing

CHAPTER THREE

Yes, But...

"We are what we repeatedly do.
Excellence, then, is not an act, but a habit."

– Aristotle

OK, I can hear you groaning over there: "How I wish I could believe that reflective practice could really offer me all the benefits you are talking about and also believe that I would be able to do it!"

Let's take your concerns one at a time.

It's too difficult to do.

Whilst it is true that reflective practice is a skill, and like all skills, takes practice to master, the basics are easy to master. And the good news is, even doing it *a little bit* (remember the Harvard research referred to in Chapter 1?) and at a beginner's skill level will bring you benefits. It is simple to learn, complex to master.

> **Whatever you do with this, builds muscle for doing it more, and better.**

I am fairly certain you can think of examples from your own lifetime of learning where this has been true: learning to cook, learning to use a new piece of computer software, learning to drive, learning a new language, just to name a few.

Think of something at which you are skilled. Write it down.

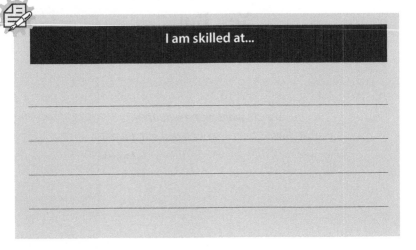

I am skilled at...

_____

_____

_____

_____

Think back to when you first started doing this thing. How good were you then? What did you have to do to build your proficiency in this activity? What do you still have to do to maintain your proficiency? The truth is that you can learn new things. It may feel awkward at first, but with learning and practice it will become more comfortable.

Learning Stages

One way of understanding this is by looking at a model that is sometimes referred to as 'the learning stages'. This model maps out four distinct stages, and it is useful to see these stages as 'steps':

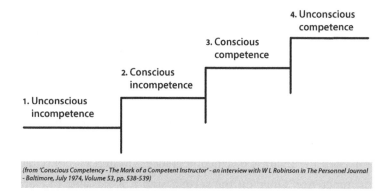

(from 'Conscious Competency - The Mark of a Competent Instructor' - an interview with W L Robinson in The Personnel Journal - Baltimore, July 1974, Volume 53, pp. 538-539)

For every new skill, we begin at the bottom, on the 'unconscious incompetence' step. We don't even know that we don't know. At this stage, we are not aware of the skill or of its relevance to us. Perhaps we have never noticed the skill in others, or perhaps we are merely blind to what it takes to develop the skill. Think about your three-year-old toddler who can 'drive' the car as well as Daddy.

Once we begin to look more closely at the skill, we begin to realise just how much work it is likely to take to develop the skill. We become 'consciously incompetent' as we become aware of how much learning and development is required in order to master the particular skill. At this point, a conscious decision needs to be made about whether to work towards progressing to the next step or not.

The next step, if we have decided to proceed, is to begin to train ourselves in the skill. Once we have engaged in the training and developed the skill, we move to the step called 'conscious competence'. We can do the skill, and we are aware of (virtually) every stage in the process. We have to concentrate and possibly follow a checklist (which may be merely mental or may be a physical checklist) in order to display the skill.

The final step in the model is 'unconscious competence' – when we are masters of the skill and can perform it without conscious awareness of the constituent parts. We are able to demonstrate proficiency in the skill without having to think about how we are doing it.

Think about your last promotion. The new tasks that came with working at a higher level likely brought awareness of moving from step 1 – unconscious incompetence – to step 2 – conscious incompetence. Once on the second step it is possible to learn the ropes of the new task, moving you on to step 3 – conscious competence. When the task becomes more 'routine' to you, you have landed on step 4 – unconscious competence.

So what does this mean for you in relation to reflective practice? Well, you have picked this book up, which suggests that you are past the 'unconscious incompetence' step. You are at least wondering whether this skill is relevant for you, and whether or not this book might contain something beneficial for you in developing your skill in this area. This suggests that you are at least on the 'conscious incompetence' step. Moving from 'conscious incompetence' to 'conscious competence' requires learning and practice. Subsequent chapters of this book will give you some information and specific skills to learn, as well as many exercises to complete and prompts to challenge yourself to practise. That will help you progress from step 2 to step 3.

Moving from 'conscious competence' to 'unconscious competence' simply requires much more practice. You know you are on step 3 when you are able to perform the skill reliably at will, albeit to start with you will need to concentrate in order to do it well. Practice is the single most effective way to move from step 3 to step 4.

One post-script to the learning steps model. It is easy to fall off the top step. Generally the fall happens if you become complacent about your skill level, and generally the fall is all the way back to the bottom step. You will have lost your high skill level, without realising it. This is a particular danger with reflective practice, as *awareness* is at the very heart of the skill. If you become complacent about your reflective abilities, you likely have become less good at reflecting!

It's touchy-feely crap.

Yes, 'reflective practice' has a reputation as something to be done in a quiet room, in a meditative mode, by someone wearing a long robe and sandals.

However, there is much science to support the benefits of reflective practice. Just one example from neuroscience is the concept of neuroplasticity. Neuroplasticity refers to the brain's ability to change with learning. This means that we can use our minds to change our brains. This implies that focusing on learning and thinking will work to effect permanent changes in our brains, which will make *doing* easier going forward as the brain will have been re-trained by our reflective practice.

It is also the case that there is proven evidence in a number of fields that reflective practice yields benefits. Although this has not been researched widely in the context of business and commercial organisations, there is evidence from a number of professional fields that reflective practice yields benefits – in psychotherapy and social work, in teaching, and in academia generally. The benefits are generally stated to include greater effectiveness and improvements in the performance of regular tasks, as well as improvements in thinking and problem solving and decision-making skills.

It's not my style.

In the last chapter you had an opportunity to identify your preferred learning style. If your learning style preference was reflector, this is probably not an objection with which you can identify. Reflecting *is* your style. What you want from this book is more methodology to follow. Feel free to skip through to the next subheading.

But if you identified a learning style preference that is something *other* than reflector, then perhaps you feel that this just isn't for you. I believe that having an underdeveloped reflector learning style will be inhibiting your best performance (I would say that, wouldn't I?!). Let's take a look at how this just might be holding you back at the moment.

If your learning style preference is either activist or pragmatist, you are likely to have a number of similar difficulties with reflective activities. You are probably more than likely to rush into action. It may be that you sometimes begin an activity with inadequate preparation and little thought for possible consequences, which means that contingency plans are often undeveloped or poorly formed. When things go wrong, the outcome is often worse than it might have been if there had been a contingency plan already prepared. Perhaps this is something you recognise. It may also mean that you make decisions too quickly, and end up doing the 'wrong' things as the decisions have been made without consideration of some important factor.

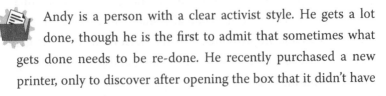 Andy is a person with a clear activist style. He gets a lot done, though he is the first to admit that sometimes what gets done needs to be re-done. He recently purchased a new printer, only to discover after opening the box that it didn't have

the capability of printing from his tablet. He'd simply assumed that it would. This meant several hours wasted, packing up the inadequate-for-his-purposes printer, taking the box to the post office, reordering a different printer, and waiting (again) for the printer to arrive.

You may find it difficult – or unpleasant – to pause during or after an activity to review your experiences and identify lessons learned. This means that the learning you *do* extract from your experiences is likely to be more ad hoc and more superficial than if your reviews were deeper, more deliberate and focused. It also means that history is likely to keep repeating itself, with similar 'errors' being made time and again.

Vijay, a director in a large accountancy firm, has a pragmatist style. He is the first to admit that he is rushed off his feet. Many external pressures conspire to ensure that he has little time for anything other than 'doing' what needs to be done. As a result of a coaching session we had, Vijay committed to spending at least 15 minutes a week (yes, just 15 minutes a week) reviewing his experiences of the week with a specific focus on extracting learning from them. He asked himself just one question: 'What is the most significant thing I can learn from my experiences this week?'

Though Vijay noted some improvements even after the first week of taking this 'time out', within a month he had his first major success as a result of the new habit. He noticed something that, left unattended, would have created a major problem for one of his largest clients. He attributed this noticing *directly* to the new habit.

It is likely that you are impatient with collecting data or reading about things which could be relevant to your work, unless (perhaps) you can see a clear practical application for the data or the reading at the current time. This means that you are likely to miss opportunities to expand your perspective or trigger creative thoughts from unexpected sources.

You may also find other people's experiences to have little relevance to your own. While it is true that no one else will have had *exactly* the same experience as you, it may be that with some reflection you could uncover from them insights into *your* experience. Instead of doing this, however, you are more likely to dismiss them quickly. This means that you are sometimes in the position of making unnecessary mistakes and reinventing wheels.

If your preference was as a theorist, it is likely that you are already spending a considerable amount of time thinking about what you are doing. However, it is likely that the thinking you are doing is focused more on abstract conceptualisation than on concrete experiences or active experimentation. Thinking – and learning – that is not linked to action may well be interesting, but in today's fast-paced competitive environments it may well not always be useful enough. You undoubtedly want to leverage your scarce thinking time for maximum advantage. It is important, therefore, to spend your thinking time where it will produce the most benefit.

Even more significantly, your thinking is likely to focus on achieving a perfect logical conclusion – discarding any subjective responses and attempting to resolve any ambiguity. We could argue that ambiguity has become a *certain* aspect of modern organisational life, and therefore it is necessary to find a way to work with it. Moreover, subjective responses are at the absolute heart of good reflective practice. I am not arguing against objectivity and logicality – merely for the inclusion of subjectivity in good reflective thinking.

For you, as a theorist, the crucial style adjustments are to develop the capacity for lateral thinking – allowing yourself to jump to a new idea without a complete logical chain – and accepting the benefit of your subjective responses. You could think of this as trusting your intuition more. In addition, it will be good to ensure that your thinking always includes a focus on 'so what?' It is fine – and indeed necessary for extracting maximum learning – to spend time on the abstract thinking that helps you assimilate new information. What is also necessary at some point in the process is to tie that thinking back into reviews of specific past and plans for specific future concrete experiences.

Next time you are gathering information to support making a decision, ask for advice from someone you initially consider to be totally irrelevant. Turn off your 'yes, but...' reflex. Consider what the source is saying, and see how you can use this to extend your own perspective. If you are thinking about reorganising your team, ask a personal trainer at the gym. If you are thinking about new technology, ask someone who doesn't have a smartphone. If you are thinking about a pitch to a new customer, ask someone who knows nothing about your business. Imagine following their advice: what could happen, what could it lead to?

Whatever your underlying learning style preference, developing your reflector learning style will have many benefits for you.

So how can you develop your reflective capacity in order to obtain those benefits?

I don't know how to begin to become more reflective.

First it would be helpful if you acknowledge what stops you from being more reflective in the first place. Some common reasons people give include:

Being short of time to plan or think

Preferring to move quickly from one activity to another

Being impatient for action

Reluctance to listen carefully and analytically to others

Reluctance to write things down

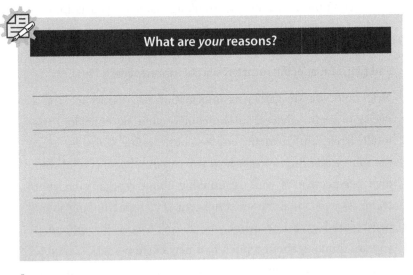

What are *your* reasons?

Reflectivity Enhancers

Thinking back to the earlier section on 'competing commitments' we might conclude that if you *really* wanted to begin, you would. Or perhaps it is simply the case that you don't know how to begin. Here are some practical activities that could be a way to make a start.

- ☼ Keep a diary for a week. Every day write down an account of what happened during the day. Think about what happened and identify a 'theme' for each day or each part of each day. Be sure to record the themes in the diary. At the end of the week, reflect on the week as a whole and see what conclusions you come to about the events of the week.

- ☼ After an important meeting or event, push yourself to spend some time reviewing it. What went well? What went less well? What would you want to do differently next time?

- ☼ Copy Vijay's habit – spend 15 minutes a week asking yourself just one key question. His was: 'What is the most significant thing I can learn from my experiences this week?' What would yours be?

- ☼ Notice the details of people's behaviour at a meeting (you could do this by watching a television programme if you would rather do it outside work). Make notes about how much time individual people speak, who interrupts whom, how often the chair summarises, etc. Also notice the non-verbals. When do people gesture? What sort of gestures do they use? What responses do you observe in others when people are gesturing?

- ☼ Identify an important decision you need to make. Identify at least five possible actions. Take time to produce balanced arguments for and against each of the actions.

- ☼ Carry on reading this book, and commit to doing at least one exercise or activity in each chapter as you go along.

> **The activity I am going to do in order to increase my reflectivity is ...**
>
> _____
>
> _____
>
> _____
>
> _____
>
> _____

It takes too much time.

This is one of the most frequent reasons cited for not spending time reflecting. Let me ask you: how much time is 'too much' time? For most thinking people, it isn't a matter of not investing *any* time, it is more a question of how much reward is required for the time invested.

Think about the Spectrum of Reflectivity we discussed in Chapter 1. You want to be sure that the time you invest in thinking is spent thinking about the right things.

You need to be sure that the time you invest can produce measurably improved results. If you absolutely knew that you would get these measurably improved outcomes from investing time in reflective thinking, and if you knew that the benefit of those improved outcomes was worth significantly more than the value of the time invested in this focused thinking, I am sure you would make the effort to invest the time. I can give you plenty of examples of such benefit from other people's lives, and indeed you will find examples throughout this book. But I do believe that the most persuasive evidence for you will be examples that come *from your own experience*. And the best way to generate those examples is to dive in and get started.

I need to keep my focus on results.

Exactly!

That is likely to be precisely what you will be thinking about. The purpose of this reflective thinking is to capitalise on your thinking time. How can you be sure you are getting the absolute best outcomes unless you are thinking carefully about what you are doing, taking every opportunity to capitalise on those things that are working well, and to mitigate against what isn't working so well? You are likely to want to say that you leverage virtually all of the resources you have at your disposal when you carry out your work. You want to use the right people in the right place at the right time doing the right tasks for the right reasons.

There is a danger that you infer from what I'm saying that not doing reflective thinking means you aren't doing *any* thinking. I absolutely don't mean that. I am sure you do a fair amount of thinking. You wouldn't be as successful as you are if you didn't. What I am suggesting, though, is that you might think differently, that you might use a specific structure to help you think things through with a particular focus, and that if you do that, your business results will improve.

I know I should do this – I've heard it before – but I just can't seem to make it a habit.

Instilling new habits is hard. Habits take time to stick.

"If you are going to achieve excellence in big things, you develop the habit in little matters."

– Colin Powell

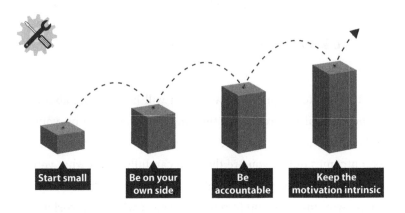

| Start small | Be on your own side | Be accountable | Keep the motivation intrinsic |

Habit Builder

Follow these steps to build a new habit.

Start small. Introduce the new habit a little bit at a time.

This has two benefits. One of the easiest ways to sabotage a new habit is by requiring yourself to go from a standing start to full-blown race speed in one immediate burst.

The other benefit is that studies have shown that when we don't meet our target, we are psychologically more likely to say "what the hell" and abandon the desired behaviour completely. (See 'The What the Hell Effect' by Winonan Cochray and Abraham Tesser in *Striving and Feeling. Interactions Among Goals, Affect and Self-Regulation,* edited by Leonard Martin and Abraham Tesser.)

Be on your own side. Support your efforts.

Turn *down* the volume on the voice of your inner critic. At the same time, turn *up* the volume on the voice that tells you that doing your best (in all the circumstances) is enough.

Be accountable. Declare your intentions, at least to yourself.

Maybe being accountable to yourself is enough. And maybe not. In any case, declare your intentions. Make them specific. Acquisitive goals – positively framed goals – are easier to achieve than inhibitive goals – getting rid of something. (Think AA: number of days sober [acquisitive] versus don't drink [inhibitive].)

Keep the motivation intrinsic. Do it because *you* want to.

This simply means do it because *you* want to and *you* can see the benefits that will accrue to you, *not* because someone else (me?) tells you it is a good idea.

So if you are ready, let's move on to the practical map, to EDGE-it.

KEY POINTS

There are many protests you can raise against building
the habit of focused, reflective thinking.
On investigation, they don't hold up.

✿

Whatever your preferred learning/communication
style, there are specific activities you can do to help you
become more reflective.

✿

New skills need to be learned and practised before
we can really call them our own. It is possible
to build new habits.

✿

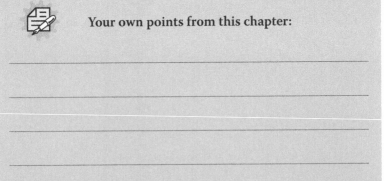

Your own points from this chapter:

_____

_____

_____

_____

_____

KEY TOOLS
INTRODUCED IN THIS CHAPTER

Learning Stages

✿

Reflectivity Enhancers

✿

Habit Builder

PART 2

The Practical Map

"He who learns but does not think, is lost.

*He who thinks but does not learn
is in great danger."*

– Confucius

Better Thinking for Better Results

CHAPTER FOUR

Representing a way of Noticing and Thinking that can be used in Virtually any Situation

I hope by now you have accepted the case for reflective thinking generally, and also identified some of your personal hoped-for benefits and answered some of your own personal objections. So now it is time to introduce you to the practical process.

I have developed a multi-part model that provides the map of the territory. I have already said that other maps already exist in other contexts. In education, for example, there have been many books written which explain the benefits of reflective practice for both teaching and learning, and many maps have been developed to explain to teachers (especially student teachers, it appears) how to be reflective, and why this is helpful for them and their students.

I think you need a process of your own, to focus you towards the operational benefits you can accrue as a result of acquiring a practice of reflection. A 'purpose-built' process, by being appropriate to your own context, will help keep you focused on the most important things at every stage.

Introducing EDGE-it: reflective practice for operational benefit

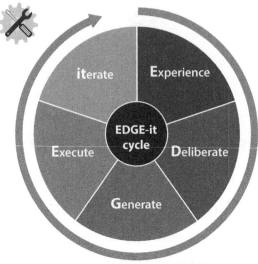

EDGE-it

This is a purpose-built process that can be applied in commercial situations, and other organisational settings. EDGE-it is a process which, when followed, brings new learning, more focused actions, improved results. Even the very name will keep you sharp!

EDGE-it can be applied in three different time zones: **in the past**, after the fact; **in the present**, in the moment; and **for the future**, forward planning. How you use the model will vary slightly from time zone to time zone. For now, however, we can take this as the basic model, and we will look at necessary time zone adjustments a little later. The general principles are the same in all three time zones.

So, let's look at the various stages of the process. Alongside the description of the basic model is a worked example.

The FIRST STAGE is E – EXPERIENCE

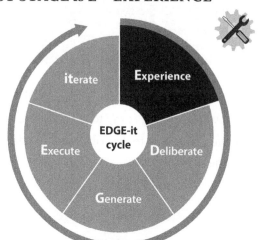

This is a chance to look at the actual **Experience**. In this stage of the process you will be looking at and describing exactly what *is*, answering numerous factual questions. What is happening? Who is involved? How is it the same as or different from other situations? You will add in 'noticing' that goes beyond the most obvious, adding in the noticing of cognitive, affective and somatic responses to the Experience.

> **At the end of this stage you will have a good awareness of the actual Experience.**

We start by carefully noticing the Experience. You really need to notice as much as you possibly can about your Experience. You need to look at it carefully. Why would we do that? Being clear about your Experience, whether it has happened in the past, is happening now, or is something you would like to Experience in the future, gives you more control over what happens next, and therefore more influence on the outcomes.

> ## "Knowledge is power"
> (commonly attributed to Francis Bacon)

There are two aspects to the Experience stage of EDGE-it. The first is preparing yourself, getting *ready* to really notice. The second is actually *noticing*, being able to describe to a high degree of detail, what the Experience is.

Jason's Story

This high-level example is intended to help clarify the basic stages of EDGE-it. In Part 3 of the book, we will spend much more time on the details of each stage, going into significantly more detail and exploring the nuances more deeply. For now, let's just look at the essence of EDGE-it.

Jason decided to apply **EDGE-it** to his last promotion interview, which was a precursor to an assessment day.

EXPERIENCE – *where the goal is to create a good awareness of the actual Experience.*

The interview was with a panel of three assessors. Jason had arrived in plenty of time, and was more or less in his desired state of calmly confident, though he did get the occasional adrenalin rush while he was waiting to be called by the panel. Reflecting on the Experience afterwards, he noticed that he had developed a better rapport with one of the assessors than the other two. He also noticed that he felt more fully himself when he was answering the panel's questions, even though they were very challenging, than he did when he was delivering a prepared statement he had been told to bring to the interview.

The SECOND STAGE is D – DELIBERATE

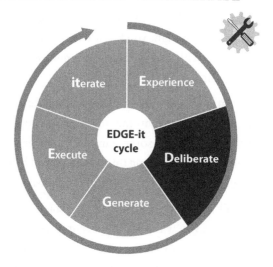

In the second stage of the process, you will **Deliberate**. It is in this stage that you will begin to try to understand exactly the meaning of what is happening. Questions you will be asking in this stage encourage you to go deeper than surface description, looking for what the Experience means to you, and thinking about what learning you'd like to extract from the situation.

> **At the end of this stage you will have become more fully aware of the Experience, and the various implications thereof, as well as what learning(s) you want to extract from the Experience.**

Notice that the name of this stage is both de-lib'-er-it, an adjective, a describing word, as well as a verb, an action word – de-lib'-er-āte. This second stage of the process is to deliberately Deliberate on your Experience, taking time to notice as much as you can about your full response. It is important to be intentional and Deliberate about this. You need to be rigorous, and to work at it.

Paying attention to what you have noticed can deepen your awareness. This in turn can help you to shift your initial perspective. How many times have you thought you knew what was happening, only to surprise yourself with a new insight or a new understanding of a familiar situation?

If you are not naturally reflective, this may be a difficult phase. Try to stay here a little longer than initially feels comfortable. It may take you a little while to build some stamina for this process, but believe me, it will be worth it. Doing this stage well will help you focus on the right questions in the next stage of the EDGE-it process.

Indeed, you will be using questions in this stage as well. In this stage of the process you will ask yourself some probing questions. You are trying to see into all the corners of the Experience and coax out its more hidden aspects. You also want to Deliberate on what useful meaning you can make of the Experience. What learning do you want to capture?

Jason's Story

DELIBERATE – *where the goal is to become more fully aware of the Experience, make meaning from it, and decide what learning you want to extract.*

Jason's reflections helped him to see that he had related better to the first assessor he'd noticed giving encouraging non-verbal signals. He wasn't sure whether or not that assessor was the first to give that sort of signal, or whether he was just the first one Jason noticed. Partly in response to that question, Jason decided it was important to determine how to build rapport more easily and earlier with a wider selection of individuals. This was the first learning he wanted to extract.

Jason was also interested in the difference in his impact when delivering a prepared statement compared with when he was

answering questions. He realised during his reflections that this was a familiar pattern, and that he often felt quite stilted while delivering presentations, and quite energised by the unpredictability of a question and answer session. He decided that he wanted to be able to deliver prepared statements with more energy and impact. This was the second learning Jason wanted to extract.

Jason's Story

When you have done this, you are ready to move on to the third stage of the EDGE-it process, G – Generate.

The THIRD STAGE is G – GENERATE

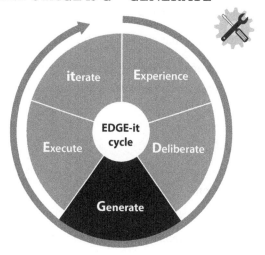

Linking learning and action is at the heart of improvement and leveraging performance. Each without the other is 'less than'.

In this third stage of the process you begin to Generate options for action, considering what you *might* do next. Creative problem solving relies on an abundance of possible solutions to any given problem, so this is the time to Generate possibilities with wild abandon. It is important to really stretch your perspective, looking at the Experience from different angles. It won't be until the next stage of the process where you will need to choose which options to go with.

> **At the end of this stage you will have a generous list of possible options for action.**

And what is it you are Generating options to do? Well, you need to Generate options to address a number of points. The first is for you to Generate ideas about how to grab the learning from this Experience. What do you want (need?) to learn? And how can you capitalise on this learning – make it count for even more? You also want to Generate ideas about how to deal with the current 'problem' or 'challenge' itself.

The key question is: What **could** I do about this now?

Remember, you don't yet have to commit to any one of these actions, so this is really 'what *could* I do?' rather than 'what *will* I do?'

Jason's Story

GENERATE – where the goal is to create a generous list of possible actions.

Jason had two learning objectives emerging from the Deliberate stage:

(1) how to build rapport more easily and earlier

(2) how to deliver prepared work with more energy and impact

His next task therefore was to Generate a list of possible options. He remembered here that it was not necessary to evaluate the options, merely to Generate them.

The options Jason came up with included:

For (1)

▶ Intentionally preparing to look for non-verbal signals early in interactions.

▶ Reading up on rapport-building skills.

▶ Practising building rapport with difficult people.

▶ Improving his memory for matching names and faces.

▶ Intentionally rotating his attention deliberately from one person to another when meeting a group of people at the same time.

For (2)

▶ Not practising any presentations, thus allowing adrenalin to give energy.

▶ Leaving some part of his presentations not considered in detail, so there would be room for some spontaneity.

▶ Including some interactivity in prepared presentations, when appropriate.

▶ Asking others he perceived as powerful presenters for tips they might have.

▶ Attending a drama workshop.

Jason's Story

The FOURTH stage is E – EXECUTE

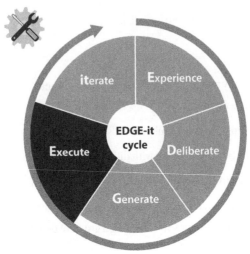

As noted, it is essential that the previous steps lead to some sort of action, so in this phase of the process you will make a choice about which option(s) to **Execute**. You will consider the options Generated about learning and action, and choose the ones that make the most sense to you. You will evaluate (another E word) the possibilities and consider your commitment to the various options, and then choose which you will Execute.

> **At the end of this stage you will have a plan of action.**

This is the stage where you need to decide what you are going to do, and actually do it. Experience-ing, Deliberate-ing and Generate-ing all need to lead to Execute-ing, to action. It is essential for action to be tied to learning. The learning itself is important; as Peter Honey once said, "Learning to learn is really important as it is the gateway to acquiring all the other skills you want to acquire." However, if we are going to insist on obtaining commercial benefit from our learning, it needs to be clearly linked to action.

This next part of the process is about doing exactly that. It is here that you evaluate which option to take and then Execute that action. The action you choose needs to make a difference – in the present, if possible, as well as in the future. And you need to be committed to the action you choose to Execute. In the subsequent chapters we will look at how to choose the action to which you feel most committed, and how to plan its execution.

EXECUTE – where the goal is to have a plan of action.

Jason then spent some time evaluating the various options he'd Generated. He considered both the difficulty of doing each particular action, as well as the impact it was likely to have on his learning objectives. Jason decided that the three things that would be best to do were:

▶ Intentionally preparing to look for non-verbal signals early in interactions.

▶ Asking others he perceived as powerful presenters for their tips.

▶ Leaving some part of his presentations not considered in detail.

He then checked his commitment against these three actions and realised that he felt fully committed to the first two, and that the third left him feeling quite nervous. He modified the action to be leaving some part of his presentations outlined in detail, and unscripted. He felt able to commit to that.

Jason's Story

The FINAL STAGE is '-it' – ITERATE

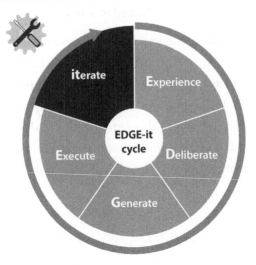

Iterate means to repeat the process. Once you have chosen the option to Execute, the action to take, the learning to embed, you will benefit from going around the cycle again. This reflective practice needs to be a habit, and only practice will help embed it as one.

> **At the end of this stage you will have gained further insight, and most importantly, you will have confidence in the rigour of your reflective practice habit.**

Each time you go around the cycle, through the stages, you deepen your learning and identify further useful actions. Even going around the process once will give you an advantage. To gain maximum benefit from EDGE, however, you need to make it a repetitive habit, iterating the process and uncovering more useful and useable learning with each iteration and identifying more pivotal actions with each circuit.

ITERATE – where the goal is to gain further insight and confidence in the habit.

Jason decided that he would review the whole EDGE-it process and its effectiveness after he attended the assessment interview. When he did so, he realised that the process had been very helpful and had given him some important improvements in his performance. He also realised that it would have been good to review earlier the EDGE-it process applied to the interview, as he believed he would have benefited from an additional action in relation to the giving of presentations. He determined that in future he would practise speaking in a more energetic style, and get feedback from colleagues about that.

Jason's Story

So there you have it, a multi-part model of reflective practice with a commercial EDGE. From working with literally thousands of executives over the past 20 years, I can see that most people don't naturally follow this cycle. What most often happens is that people

- ⚙ **Have an Experience**
- ⚙ **Skip the Deliberate step**
- ⚙ **Spend a VERY short time on Generate, enough to come up with one idea or perhaps two**
- ⚙ **Pretty much move directly to Execute, and then**
- ⚙ **Never think about it again**

Taking these short cuts often results in doing more – but doing the 'wrong' things, or doing things 'wrong'. There is much evidence to suggest that following the full cycle can help you do more of the 'right' things and do them better.

So – When can you use EDGE-it?

As mentioned above, you can use EDGE-it in three different time zones.

☼ In the past: EDGE-it works when used 'after the fact'

This is probably the situation that is most often referred to in traditional reflective practice texts. Here I am talking about using EDGE-it to reflect back on something that has already happened, in order both to extract learning from the specific situation and also to promote continuous improvement. The overall reason to apply EDGE-it to an Experience that has already occurred is to improve future performance. It is useful for leveraging *any* Experience for maximum benefit.

The key to success when applying EDGE-it after the fact is to allow a fuller exploration than you would have done before. It can still be quick – it needn't take an extremely long time (although depending on the importance of the Experience you might decide to devote a considerable amount of time to the process).

You can do this alone or with others. When you work on it on your own, it is called *intra*-personal reflection. Such reflections might include writing, structured thinking, meditating, using poetry or drawing, for example. Reflecting with others, *inter*-personal reflection, usually uses conversation or other methods for sharing thoughts with others.

In Chapter 5 you will have the opportunity to work through a specific example, applying EDGE-it after the fact. If you can't wait, feel free to turn now to page 101 .

In the present: EDGE-it works when applied 'in the moment'

How many times have you experienced what is called *'esprit d'escalier'*, a French term which means 'stairway thinking'? You are just on your way out of a meeting, or have just pressed 'send' on that email, or have just hung up the phone. You have a sense of vague dissatisfaction (or perhaps *clear* disappointment with how things have gone) and suddenly you realise just what you could have said or written which would have swung the outcome into a much more positive realm. EDGE-it can help you reduce the times when that happens.

Mindfulness is the current buzzword for this. It means being aware of the present, bringing your full awareness to the here and now. Often, meditative practices are used to support the development of mindful awareness. There is much evidence to support the assertion that such practices change the actual structure of the brain, making it even easier to return to mindful states as your practice (your brain!) develops. Intuitively, though this goes against traditional thinking about adult brain development, it makes sense that as parts of the brain are used, they develop. Why should it be any different from development of any other part of the body? You go to the gym, your muscles develop. You exercise your brain, *it* develops.

When you want to reflect in the moment, you need a process that is incredibly quick. EDGE-it can be that quick – you can run through the phases in nano-seconds. If you ever need to think on your feet, this can work for you.

We will cover this **in Chapter 6**. If you want to get started with that right now, turn to page 151 .

☼ For the future: EDGE-it works on something that hasn't happened yet

In another deviation from established academic thinking on reflective practice, you can also apply EDGE-it to something that hasn't happened yet, which you would *like* to have happen. Most powerfully, this can be used in relation to a goal you've set for yourself.

Visualising in explicit detail what you'd LIKE to Experience would be the starting point. Describe that Experience in the present tense, using what I call 'future perfect' language. It is 'future' because you use the present tense as if what is happening in the future is happening right now. It is 'perfect' because it describes what you desire to have happen. It is a way of 'standing in the future', and 'experiencing' the achievement of your goal.

Once the Experience is visualised, you can apply EDGE-it more fully. You will get a chance to do that **in Chapter 7**. If you can't wait, turn now to page 185 to begin.

It doesn't matter in which context, in which time zone, you apply EDGE-it: it can be after the fact, in the moment, or applied to something that hasn't even happened yet. Each application of EDGE-it builds muscles for future applications. You will see as you go through the rest of this book that some of the processes are the same regardless of the context.

KEY POINTS

EDGE-it is a five-stage model:

Experience – notice the actual Experience in depth

Deliberate – understand the meaning

Generate – create options for action

Execute – evaluate options and choose
which one(s) to do

iterate – repeat in some way

☼

EDGE-it was designed to be applied in an
organisational context. It is a hard-edged model, the
application of which results in improved outcomes.

☼

EDGE-it can be used in any one of three time zones:
looking at the past, after the fact; in the present, in
the moment; and for the future, forward planning.
The basic model is the same in all three time zones,
needing only limited time-zone specific adjustments.

☼

Your own points from this chapter:

_____

_____

_____

_____

_____

KEY TOOL
INTRODUCED IN THIS CHAPTER

EDGE-it

PART 3

Applying EDGE-it in Three Time Zones

This part of the book sets out how to apply EDGE-it in each of the three time zones. Each chapter is divided into two sections: the first describes the process, including some exercises you can do to apply EDGE-it to your own Experiences. The second part gives you some workbook-style pages on which you can apply EDGE-it to additional situations. You might want to photocopy the workbook pages first so that you can use them more than once.

Better Thinking for Better Results

CHAPTER FIVE

EDGE-it
After the Fact

"Life is a series of experiences, each one of which makes us bigger, even though sometimes it is hard to realize this."

– Henry Ford

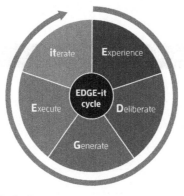

You have decided that you want to learn to apply EDGE-it 'after the fact'. Perhaps something important has happened? Perhaps you have had a less-than-desired outcome from a recent Experience? Or maybe you want to consider a high stakes past Experience which has important implications for the future?

101

The first step is to select the Experience to which you want to apply EDGE-it.

The Experience I want to apply EDGE-it to is:

\
\
\
\

I choose this Experience for EDGE-it because:

\
\
\
\

I hope that the following will result from EDGE-it:

\
\
\
\

OK, now that you have decided on an Experience, let's take the stages in order. Working through the exercises incorporated here will help you make the process your own. Remember, too, that there are workbook pages at the end of this chapter that you can use in applying EDGE-it to additional situations.

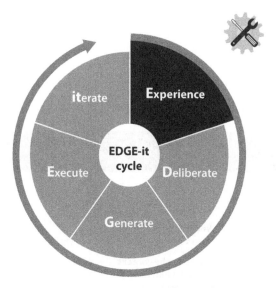

The FIRST STAGE is E – EXPERIENCE

The first step here is to describe the Experience you had. You want to describe this as fully as possible. Gather facts and feelings about the Experience and write them down.

Take your time, and write down everything you can remember about what happened. Notice as much as you can. It is here that you gather the facts of what happened and the feelings you remember having at the time. At this stage it is not about making meaning, it is purely about documenting the history. Spend some time recalling as much as you can about the Experience.

Remember that the feelings you are gathering are both about affective feelings (your emotions) and about somatic responses (physical sensations). Go back to Chapter 2 if you want a reminder about this.

When you are finished writing as much as you can about the Experience, answering the trigger questions and any others that occur to you in the process, ask yourself: What else?

See and Hear?

The focus is on three things: What did you see and hear? What did you do? What did you feel? Use the 'trigger' questions and the template opposite to help you:

Gather facts and feelings	Self	Others
See and hear?	What did I say? What did I hear others say? What was the context in which I had this experience?	Who was there? What did they say? What would they have heard me say?
Do?	At the time, how did I respond to the Experience? What did I actually do?	What did others do during the Experience?
Feel?	At the time, how did I feel - what emotions did I notice or do I remember having - about the experience I was having? How familiar did the experience feel? What did it remind me of? What body sensations did I have during the Experience?	What was the 'tone' used by others? How did I interpret that at the time?

Gather facts and feelings	Self	Others
See and hear?		
Do?		
Feel?		

Different perspectives

Remember that reflective practice goes beyond description. What begins to help extend the Experience stage beyond simple description is gathering different perspectives. This is something you can do either literally or virtually. If you are going to do it literally, consider whom else you might ask for their perspective on the Experience. Perhaps there were others with whom you shared the Experience, and you might want to ask them for their views on what happened. Or perhaps there are other people who know something about the kind of Experience you had who might be able to shed some light on the Experience from a different perspective.

Perspectives Generator

Maybe you would prefer to gather perspectives virtually. You might begin to imagine how various others would have described the situation. You can rely on real people past and present, fictional characters, people from all parts of your life. Your list might include people like:

- Your favourite manager of all time
- Your least favourite manager of all time
- Steve Jobs
- Barack Obama
- Margaret Thatcher
- Superman
- Your mother
- Sir Clive Sinclair
- Henry VIII

Who else might have a useful perspective? The idea here is to help yourself think *around and into* the Experience, and using different characters can free you to think more widely. Choose a couple of key people and write down something of how you think *they* might view your Experience.

Person, real or fictional	Perspective

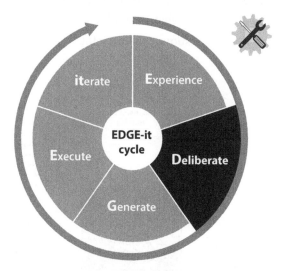

The SECOND STAGE is D – DELIBERATE

In this second stage it is important to remember that what you are trying to do is to extract all the meaning you can from the Experience, as well as identifying what it is you want to learn from the Experience. Extracting learning from Experience is a key human driver. This is an essential aspect of personal and human development.

> **He who does not learn from Experience is doomed to repeat it.**
> *Santayana*

There are a number of different methods that can help achieve your Deliberate objectives, and we are going to look at several of them.

Intrapersonal reflective writing

The first is by engaging in intrapersonal reflective writing. This is a fancy way of saying that you will work by yourself, think about the Experience, and write down what comes to you. It will be important to know what to think about – and this is where additional trigger questions can be useful.

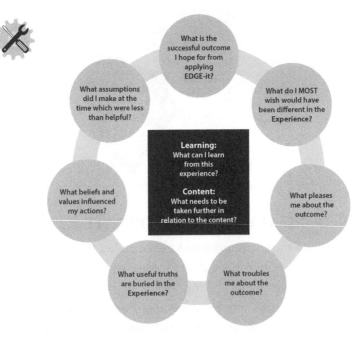

What is the successful outcome I hope for from applying EDGE-it?

What assumptions did I make at the time which were less than helpful?

What do I MOST wish would have been different in the Experience?

Learning: What can I learn from this experience?

Content: What needs to be taken further in relation to the content?

What pleases me about the outcome?

What beliefs and values influenced my actions?

What useful truths are buried in the Experience?

What troubles me about the outcome?

Learning/Content Question Wheel

The questions you ask yourself in this stage are designed to help you focus on the relevant learning. Begin anywhere, take the questions in any order, revisit questions. The questions here are merely examples. The questions themselves are not the process, they are merely stimuli for your thinking. The focus is on the two points in the centre of the circle. Deliberate on your Experience. Go as deep as you can.

Interpersonal reflection

It may be that you would prefer to engage in *interpersonal* reflection. This means that the reflection takes place between two or more people. So perhaps you would organise a conversation about the Experience. You may already do this to some extent. They may be called post-action reviews, or post-mortems. The key to success in this stage is making sure that you are thinking about the right things. It is absolutely crucial that you Deliberate on the Experience, and deepen your awareness of the Experience. Conversations with others may be able to help you here.

Reflect with/converse with these people	Perspective gained

In addition to writing or talking about your Experience, it is also possible to Deliberate using other means. These can be done on your own or in conjunction with others. Here are some examples.

Drawing

One possibility is to use drawing. Drawing accesses a different part of the brain than writing words. This may therefore give you access to new perspectives, and deepening awareness of your Experience.

 Take a moment to experiment with this. Go back to the Experience you wanted to EDGE-it. You should already have a very detailed description of the Experience, which you created in the first stage of the process. Now, on the blank page opposite, draw your Experience. This is not about the artwork, this is about using a less familiar methodology to deepen your awareness of the Experience. Draw whatever comes to mind. Use whatever colours you have to hand. Make it as realistic or impressionistic as you like. Try to draw without thinking too much. Perhaps use your non-dominant hand. This can help access areas of your brain that are used less often.

When you have finished, step back and take a look at what you have drawn. What do you notice? Look at the relative sizes of different objects. Look at the different weights of any lines you have drawn. Look at the relative positions of any of the items in your drawing. What is the general impression you get when you look at the drawing? What feelings do you have when you look at the drawing? What does it remind you of?

Perhaps ask someone else to look at the drawing. (Are you brave enough?) Ask them what they notice about it. See if you can listen to what they say and see what meaning you make of what they say.

AN EXAMPLE:

Dora was a youth leader who was having difficulty with one of her managers. In a coaching session she decided to draw a picture of the relationship she had with this manager. After spending just 30 seconds with a pen and piece of A4 paper, she had drawn this (included with Dora's permission):

The first things she noticed when she'd finished drawing were that the figure representing herself didn't have any ears and she felt that the manager was *much* bigger than she herself was. During a short discussion of the drawing, Dora realised that she needed to listen to her manager more carefully, and at the same time reclaim some of her personal power. Dora said that before doing the drawing she would have said that she was afraid that if she invited comments from the manager she would be relinquishing her personal power. The drawing helped her to see that fear more clearly, and to realise that it would be possible to listen from a position of power. Her next task was to determine how to make that happen.

Poetry and Quotations

Another possibility is to use poetry or quotations to Deliberate on your experience. Again, remind yourself of the Experience you had. Take a minute to re-acquaint yourself with the details of the Experience. Using poems and quotations is a kind of paradigm shift, allowing your mind to consider possibilities that would not have occurred to you when thinking about the situation more directly.

Now have a look at some of these poems and quotations. Choose one, and spend a few minutes thinking about what it means to you.

If

By Rudyard Kipling

If you can keep your head when all about you Are losing theirs and blaming it on you, If you can trust yourself when all men doubt you, But make allowance for their doubting too;

If you can wait and not be tired by waiting, Or being lied about, don't deal in lies, Or being hated, don't give way to hating, And yet don't look too good, nor talk too wise:

If you can dream—and not make dreams your master; If you can think—and not make thoughts your aim; If you can meet with Triumph and Disaster And treat those two impostors just the same;

If you can bear to hear the truth you've spoken Twisted by knaves to make a trap for fools, Or watch the things you gave your life to, broken, And stoop and build 'em up with worn-out tools:

If you can make one heap of all your winnings And risk it on one turn of pitch-and-toss, And lose, and start again at your beginnings And never breathe a word about your loss;

If you can force your heart and nerve and sinew To serve your turn long after they are gone, And so hold on when there is nothing in you Except the Will which says to them: 'Hold on!'

If you can talk with crowds and keep your virtue, Or walk with Kings—nor lose the common touch, If neither foes nor loving friends can hurt you, If all men count with you, but none too much;

If you can fill the unforgiving minute With sixty seconds' worth of distance run, Yours is the Earth and everything that's in it,

And—which is more—you'll be a Man, my son!

Source: A Choice of Kipling's Verse (1943)

The Field

Rumi

Out beyond ideas of wrongdoing and rightdoing there is a field.
I'll meet you there.

When the soul lies down in that grass the world is too full to talk about.

On Children
By Kahlil Gibran

Your children are not your children.

They are the sons and daughters of Life's longing for itself.

They come through you but not from you,

And though they are with you yet they belong not to you.

You may give them your love but not your thoughts,

For they have their own thoughts.

You may house their bodies but not their souls,

For their souls dwell in the house of tomorrow,

which you cannot visit, not even in your dreams.

You may strive to be like them,

but seek not to make them like you.

For life goes not backward nor tarries with yesterday.

You are the bows from which your children

as living arrows are sent forth.

The archer sees the mark upon the path of the infinite,

and He bends you with His might

that His arrows may go swift and far.

Let your bending in the archer's hand be for gladness;

For even as He loves the arrow that flies,

so He loves also the bow that is stable.

The Road Not Taken
By Robert Frost

Two roads diverged in a yellow wood,
And sorry I could not travel both
And be one traveler, long I stood
And looked down one as far as I could
To where it bent in the undergrowth;

Then took the other, as just as fair,
And having perhaps the better claim,
Because it was grassy and wanted wear;
Though as for that the passing there
Had worn them really about the same,

And both that morning equally lay
In leaves no step had trodden black.
Oh, I kept the first for another day!
Yet knowing how way leads on to way,
I doubted if I should ever come back.

I shall be telling this with a sigh
Somewhere ages and ages hence:
Two roads diverged in a wood, and I—
I took the one less traveled by,
And that has made all the difference.

Using the table below, make a few notes about the thoughts and feelings you have when you read your selection.

Poem or quotation chosen	Thoughts and feelings engendered by reading the poem or quotation

Now go back to your Experience. Extend your work on the table by reflecting on the thoughts and feelings engendered by the selection itself, and how this might relate to your Experience.

Thoughts and feelings engendered by reading the poem or quotation	Thoughts and feelings translated into the context of the Experience
(as above, in the first step of the process)	

Sanjay was a finance director who had recently been promoted from a regional board to the national board of directors of his organisation. He had received feedback that he needed to be more directive and assertive now that he was on the main board. He believed this personal transformation to be critical for his success, but believed that it would require a personality transplant – something he was not surprisingly unwilling to undergo! One day in a coaching session we decided to use poetry to try to unlock this conflict. On scanning a selection of poems, Sanjay was drawn to 'On Children' by Kahlil Gibran. He strongly identified with his role as father, and realised that in that role he was indeed able to be assertive and directive – it was his sense of responsibility that enabled it. Once he had identified 'responsibility' as the key to unlocking his assertiveness, he was able to apply this to his role as main board director, and the necessary transformation became doable.

These methods can work because they free us from the perceived requirement to be logical and sequential in deepening our thinking. Deliberating is not always a linear process, and it can be good to free ourselves from the tyranny of linearity. For example, you may well be aware of the technique called 'mind mapping'. This system, developed by Tony Buzan, is a powerful graphic technique. It combines words, colour and images in a way that allows the output of the brain to be translated on to paper in a way that generates clearer thinking. To read more about this technique, check out **www.tonybuzan.com.**

The key to successful Deliberating is to allow your mind to do its work. Use whatever prompts you find helpful – poetry, drawing, prompt questions, mind mapping, just to name a few – and keep going until you have extracted the most meaning possible from your Experience.

Remember that the two key questions at the heart of the Deliberate stage are:

LEARNING: *What can I learn from this Experience?*

CONTENT: *What needs to be taken further in relation to the content?*

 Take some time to record here the preliminary answers you have to these two questions in relation to the Experience to which you are applying EDGE-it.

LEARNING: What can I learn from this Experience?

_____

_____

_____

_____

_____

_____

_____

CONTENT: What needs to be taken further in relation to the content?

_____

_____

_____

_____

_____

_____

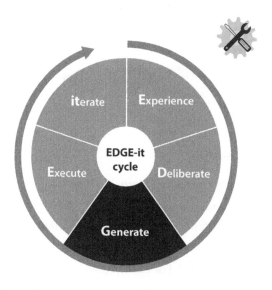

The THIRD STAGE is G – GENERATE

So now you have really captured the key facts and feelings about the Experience, and taken some time to Deliberate on the Experience, which served to deepen your understanding of what happened, as well as to clarify your learning objectives. The next stage in the process is to Generate. The main focus here is to Generate options for action.

Most of the established wisdom on creative problem solving suggests that the best solutions come when you Generate a large number of possible solutions. So we are aiming for a big list. Much problem solving in the commercial world is unfortunately done using an 'either/or' methodology: 'I could do this or I could do that'. This severely limits your chances of finding the best options.

To EDGE your Experience most powerfully and successfully, you need to Generate a wide range of possible options. Consider your next steps from many angles.

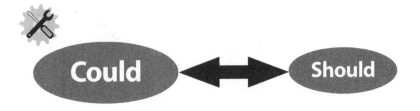

Could or Should?

One of the key questions here is: What could I have done differently? You may be used to a slightly different version of this question, that is: What *should* I have done differently? This looks similar, and is actually quite a different question. The psychology of *should* is not helpful. For example:

- ☼ *'Should'* thinking usually comes from judgements of others or general pressures of society, rather than internal personal desires

- ☼ *'Should'* thinking can come from comparing ourselves with others, often unfavourably, with the result that we can feel inadequate

- ☼ *'Should'* thinking can result in worry and anxiety, as we become concerned that we are somehow not enough as we are

- ☼ *'Should'* thinking can create a sense of obligation and duty that can weigh heavily on us

'Could' thinking is much more positive and yields many more options than *'should'.* Try substituting 'could' in your 'should' sentences and see how liberating it can be.

We are aiming for a positive and creative approach to learning. Beware therefore of blaming – even if (especially if!) the only person you are blaming is yourself.

You will undoubtedly be familiar with the idea generating methodology referred to as brainstorming which works on the principle of Generating ideas without censoring or evaluation.

What other techniques to Generate ideas do you already know?

- Brainstorming
-
-
-
-
-
-

Here are a couple of techniques you may not have tried before.

Random word

Choose any book you have to hand. It doesn't matter if it is fiction or non-fiction, reference book or poetry. Open the book to any page, and without looking at the words, place your finger on any word in the book. Then, use that word to freely associate and see what ideas might spring from it.

A coaching client who was recently trying to determine how best to prepare for an upcoming meeting used this technique. The word pointed to was monopoly. From this, she thought about board games and the significance of the positioning of properties on the various spaces in Monopoly the game. Working with this, she realised that where she placed herself in the room to make her presentation was going to be important. It was also important where others were located, and each of the others had meaning for her in terms of her presentation – some were supporters, some would be costly to land on, some would be beneficial to land on. From this one word, an entire successful strategy was born.

Concept fan

This was an idea originated by the great thinker Edward de Bono. It is designed specifically to broaden your perspective on a problem in order to Generate a wider range of possible solutions than was originally possible. On a large piece of paper draw a square and write in the square the problem you are trying to solve. To the right of this, on separate 'spokes', write down possible solutions.

Let's say you want to improve your work-life balance. A first attempt might look like this:

If this doesn't give you quite the solution you are looking for, however, you can take a step back, and insert a new 'problem' to the left of the original one. In our example, it might then look something like this:

If this still doesn't give you the answer you really want, you can move to the left again. In our example, the way to solve the problem may be to change something *before* the workload gets to you. It might be that actually it is a *good* thing that the workload is increasing, it is just that it is not a good thing that it is coming to you. Saying 'no' and delegating might help the situation, but not at its root. The root might be to improve the matching of demands and resources. Then the diagram might look like this:

You can see here that you have a different range of options, addressing a deeper level issue, and therefore more likely to solve the problem at source than the options originally Generated would have done.

In any case, whatever technique you use, creative problem solving suggests having an abundance of possibilities. To do this, you will need to leave your internal censor/critic at home. Each time you hear your inner critic's voice, try saying: 'Thank you for sharing, now go away!'

At this point in the process, you do not have to commit to any of the options you Generate, so you can afford to be wide ranging. When you think you are finished, ask yourself: What else? Try to Generate a very much longer list of options than you initially thought possible. Aim for at least 30 – and no, that's not a typo! And remember to include the question: What happens if I don't do anything?

 ### Quantity over Quality

List opposite the options you have created in the Generate stage of the EDGE-it process:

QUANTITY > QUALITY

Options for achieving the objectives determined in Deliberate include:

1 _____
_____
2 _____
_____
3 _____
_____
4 _____
_____
5 _____
_____
6 _____
_____
7 _____
_____
8 _____
_____
9 _____
_____
10 _____
_____
11 _____
_____
12 _____
_____
13 _____
_____
14 _____
_____
15 _____
_____

16 _____
_____
17 _____
_____
18 _____
_____
19 _____
_____
20 _____
_____
21 _____
_____
22 _____
_____
23 _____
_____
24 _____
_____
25 _____
_____
26 _____
_____
27 _____
_____
28 _____
_____
29 _____
_____
30 _____
_____

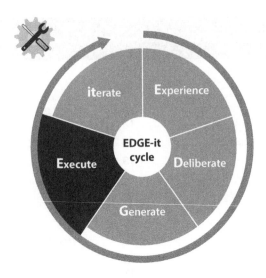

The FOURTH stage is E – EXECUTE

This stage is the one in which you evaluate which option to take and Execute that action. Experiencing, Deliberating and Generating need to lead to Executing in order to capitalise on the time invested in the process.

You may have noticed that I have sneaked in an extra E there – evaluate. It is important for the creative process in Generate that the right-brain production of options is free from the left-brain process of evaluation. Only once the creative process has been completed is it appropriate to evaluate.

How do you typically choose what to do? There are many techniques to help with choosing an action. Here are just a few – which of these are you familiar with?

- Cost benefit
- Pros and cons
- Let the universe decide

- Let my internal critic decide
- According to what feels good in the moment
- The way my mother would want me to
- Struggle and suffer

None of these is inherently superior to any other. It is absolutely impossible to know if you have made a good decision about anything – however it works out, it is not possible to know whether another decision would have been better. The only thing you can know is whether or not you made the decision well. That means that you need to evaluate your options carefully and choose a course of action that makes sense to you at the time of choosing.

For whatever decision you have in hand, explore your preferred way of making the decision. What kinds of things would you need to consider? Then try another one, perhaps the one that feels the most absurd. And another, perhaps the one that feels most connected to your preferred way. And another. And another. It can be useful to create a choice wheel, labelled with different ways of choosing, and consider the decision from each of the different ways. Ask yourself: What information would I need, and what would my choice be?

What information will I need?

What will my choice be?

Once you have an idea about how to choose from the options you Generated in the previous stage of EDGE-it, it is time to begin to develop a plan of action. You are ready now to evaluate and Execute your chosen option(s) One simple tool that can be used in planning, to help you choose options to convert to actions, is a 2x2 matrix of ease and impact.

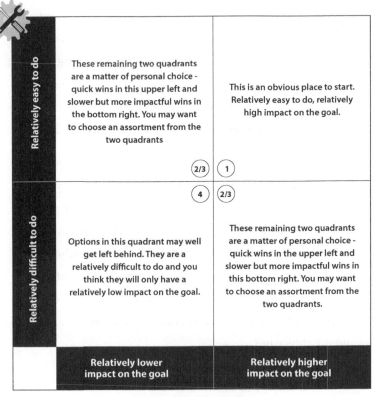

Ease/Impact Matrix

Take each of your options and evaluate them as to either relatively easy for you to do or relatively difficult for you to do. This is the first cut, and determines whether the option goes above the horizontal line (relatively easier) or below it (relatively more difficult).

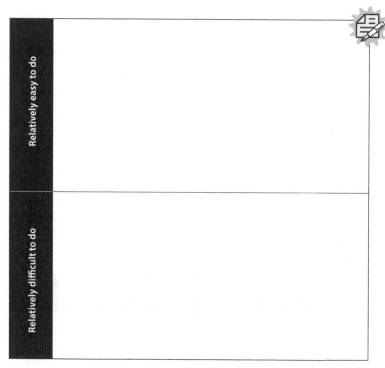

Once you have done the first cut, sort the options again, taking the relatively easy ones first and deciding whether they have a relatively lower or relatively higher impact on the goal. Relatively lower impact options go in the left quadrant, relatively higher impact options in the right. This is for the top half of the matrix.

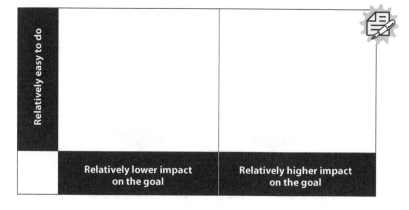

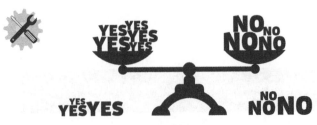

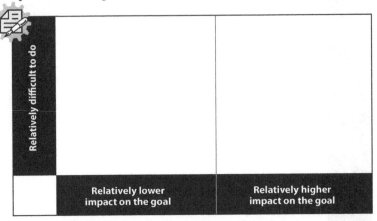

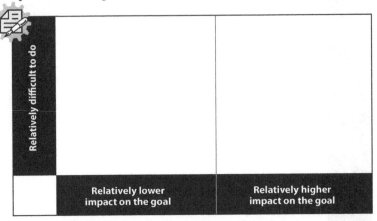

Then repeat that sorting with the options below the horizontal line, the more difficult options. Those with relatively lower impact on the goal go in the left quadrant, relatively higher impact options in the right. This is for the bottom half of the matrix.

Now your options are sorted into the four quadrants. (One good way of doing this is to put your options on to sticky notes so you can move them around easily.)

In any case, once you have sorted your options into categories, it is likely to be obvious to you what to do. Be sure you have identified the first step to take, and double check that the action you choose is pointed towards your goal. Ask yourself: *Is what I am choosing to do taking me closer to my goal?*

Once you have evaluated your options, you need to make your final choice. This is the option you are going to Execute. The best choice to Execute is one to which you feel committed.

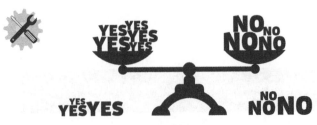

Hidden Aspects

One important step as part of testing your commitment is to look at what the more hidden aspects are to each choice. Every time you say 'yes' to something you are saying 'no' to something else. For everything you say 'no' to, you are saying 'yes' to something else.

For example, Joseph wanted to sort out his personal finances. Well, he sort of wanted to sort them out. By deciding to look carefully at his current financial position he was saying 'yes' to:

- ⚙ **The risk of facing bad news**
- ⚙ **Spending time on financial matters**
- ⚙ **Increasing his financial awareness**
- ⚙ **Clarity about money**

In this same decision, he would be saying 'no' to:

- ⚙ **Uncertainty and unease about finances**
- ⚙ **His apparent inability to sort this out**
- ⚙ **Uninformed financial decision making**
- ⚙ **His (uneasy) 'truce' with his partner**
- ⚙ **Blissful (?) ignorance about his financial position**

Once he was clear about these matters, the aspect that concerned him most was his 'truce' with his partner. He decided to tackle this head-on, and once the necessary conversation had been conducted, they were free to look carefully at their financial position.

Do this now for yourself. Look at the actions you are considering. Pay attention to what you are saying 'yes' to and what you are saying 'no' to.

Action being considered	The 'yes' this represents	The 'no' this represents

And now you need to check your level of commitment.

1	2	3	4	5	6	7	8	9	10

Scale of Commitment

On a scale of 1–10, where 1 is 'I might do it but probably not', and 10 is 'I will definitely do it – can hardly wait to get to it', how committed do you feel? If your answer is less than 10, you have not chosen the right action. You need to go back and look again. Perhaps the action is going in the right direction, but is merely a bit too big. Break down the action into smaller pieces, shorter steps, until you have the step to which you feel committed at level 10.

Also be sure to include 'by when'. Hold yourself accountable.

The actions I commit to doing are:

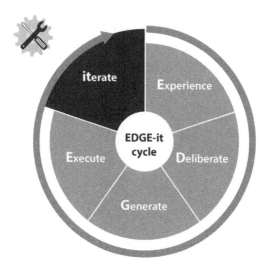

And now the '-it' – ITERATE

By this stage in the process you will have applied EDGE-it to something that happened in the past.

E - EXPERIENCE – exploring the facts and feelings of what happened.

D- DELIBERATE – deepening the awareness about what happened and identifying opportunities for learning.

G- GENERATE – identifying the actual pivotal learning from the Experience, and producing options for next steps.

E - EXECUTE – evaluating the options, and your level of commitment, and choosing the one(s) to Execute.

Now it is time to repeat the cycle. Iterate. Consider how important the Experience was to you. Consider how important the learning is that emerges from this process. Consider how significant the actions are.

Go around the cycle again. Try to notice what you have missed. Look at it from a slightly 'higher up the mountain' position. What patterns are there? How familiar is this Experience? What options are you *not* considering? What defensiveness is there in what you have learned from this Experience?

_____

_____

_____

_____

Go around the cycle again. This time, focus on the *process* of reflecting, rather than the content of the Experience. You could apply EDGE-it to the Experience of doing the reflecting:

E – Describe the Experience you had when you applied EDGE-it. What happened? What was it like? What thoughts and feelings were evoked?

D – Which stages of applying EDGE-it were harder? Which were easier? How do you understand that? What do you want to learn from your Experience of applying EDGE-it?

G –How could you make that learning happen? What could you do to make your next EDGE-it Experience even better?

E – Which option will you choose to make your next EDGE-it Experience even better? What action will you take? And when? What can you do *now* to make your next EDGE-it Experience better, and what will wait until you next apply EDGE-it?

Finally, make sure you do the action or actions you have chosen. If you find yourself procrastinating, go back to E – Evaluate and Execute. Think again about your options. What is stopping you from executing the option you chose? What other option could you choose to which you could commit at a 10? What would be better about that option than the one you initially chose?

Well done. You have extracted learning from your Experience and taken at least one relevant action as a result of applying EDGE-it to what happened.

KEY POINTS

E – EXPERIENCE. A full description of the Experience you have had. Remember to notice at three levels: cognitive, affective, somatic. Extend your perspective.

✿

D - DELIBERATE. Extract all the meaning you can. Key questions are: 'What can I learn?' and 'What needs to be taken forward?' Include non-traditional methods, such as drawing or poetry, for example, of extracting as much meaning as you can.

✿

G – GENERATE. Remember it is about quantity, not quality at this stage. Go wide with your choices. No evaluation at this stage.

✿

E – EXECUTE. There are many ways to evaluate your options. And what is key is identifying an option or options to which you can actually commit.

✿

it – ITERATE. Two choices here. Go around again and pick up what has been missed. And/or go around again with a focus on the process of applying EDGE-it.

✿

Your own points from this chapter:

_____

_____

_____

_____

KEY TOOLS
INTRODUCED IN THIS CHAPTER

Experience:
See and Hear?
Perspectives Generator

✿

Deliberate:
Learning/Content Question Wheel
Drawing
Poetry/Quotations

✿

Generate:
Could or Should
Random Word
Concept Fan
Quantity over Quality

✿

Execute:
Ease/Impact Matrix
Hidden Aspects - Saying 'Yes'/Saying 'No'
Scale of Commitment

Workbook pages for applying EDGE-it After the Fact

Make a note here of the situation in the past to which you are going to apply EDGE-it:

EXPERIENCE

The objective of this step of the process is to really describe the Experience. It is here that you gather the facts about what happened. At this stage it is not about making meaning, it is purely about gathering the facts. Spend some time recalling as much as you can about the Experience. Fill in the table below with as much as you can recall. When you have finished, ask yourself: What else?

Gather facts and feelings	Self	Others
See and hear?		
Do?		
Feel?		

Try to Generate some additional perspectives. Think about people, real or fictional, and what their perspectives could add.

Person, real or fictional	Perspective

DELIBERATE

The objective of this step of the process is to really make meaning from the Experience. Here, you really want to challenge yourself to go deeper into the Experience, broadening and deepening your perspective on it.

Begin anywhere, take the questions in any order, revisit questions. The questions here are merely examples. The questions themselves are not the process, they are merely stimuli for your thinking. The focus is on the two points in the centre of the circle. Deliberate on your Experience. Go as deep as you can.

What is the successful outcome I hope for from applying EDGE-it?

What do I MOST wish would have been different in the Experience?

What assumptions did I make at the time which were less than helpful?

Learning:
What can I learn from this experience?

Content:
What needs to be taken further in relation to the content?

What pleases me about the outcome?

What beliefs and values influenced my actions?

What useful truths are buried in the Experience?

What troubles me about the outcome?

Perhaps some interpersonal reflections would help, that is conversations with others.

Reflect with/converse with these people	Perspective gained

Consider what drawing might add...

...or the use of poetry or quotations.

Poem or quotation chosen	Thoughts and feelings engendered by reading the poem or quotation

Thoughts and feelings engendered by reading the poem or quotation	Thoughts and feelings translated into the context of the Experience
(as above, in the first step of the process)	

When you have finished, answer the two key Deliberate questions:

LEARNING: What can I learn from this Experience?

CONTENT: What needs to be taken further in relation to the content?

Generate

Objectives I take forward from Deliberate	
Learning	
Content	

The objective of this step of the process is to begin to Generate options – options for what to do next. At this stage you are *not* evaluating the options, so feel free to be as creative as you can be.

It is important at this stage to allow yourself to Generate as many options as possible. Many of us tend to restrict our thinking to 'either.../or...' thinking, which limits the chance we will find the 'best' options. However many options you Generate, always try to get a few more. Ask yourself: What else?

Options for achieving the objectives determined in Deliberate include:

1	16
2	17
3	18
4	19
5	20
6	21
7	22
8	23
9	24
10	25
11	26
12	27
13	28
14	29
15	30

EXECUTE

The objective of this step of the process is to decide what you are actually going to do. This could be either the next step, or a whole plan, or both. At this stage you need to evaluate your options and test your commitment to them.

You can do this in three steps:

1. First, take all the options you have Generated and place them into the ease/impact grid. Be sure to consider:

    What assumptions am I making that lead me to place this option in this quadrant? How do I know these assumptions are right? What else could be true?

    Move the options into different quadrants if necessary.

2. Decide what you are going to do next. You might want to consider the very next step, or, if you have loads of good ideas Generated, you may want the next step to be to make a plan, to incorporate many of the ideas you have Generated.

3. Finally, test your level of commitment to the action. Using a scale of 1–10, where 1 is 'I am not going to do this, but I had to come up with something' and 10 is 'I absolutely will do this – I can hardly wait to stop reading this book so I can make it happen', assign a number to your level of will to Execute each option.

| 1 | 2 | 3 | 4 | 5 | 6 | 7 | 8 | 9 | 10 |

The actions I commit to doing are:

ITERATE

This is to repeat, to go around again. This step of the EDGE-it cycle is useful for reflecting on the *process* of reflecting itself. Go back over the process you just completed, and apply EDGE-it to that. You could ask, for example:

- ☼ What do you notice about how you reflected?
- ☼ What did you miss?
- ☼ What did you focus on?
- ☼ What were the difficult parts?
- ☼ What was easier?
- ☼ Where were you most engaged?
- ☼ What would you like to do differently next time?
- ☼ How could you make that happen?
- ☼ What *will* you do differently next time?

This stage of EDGE-it is also useful in going back over the content. You could go back over your workings in this section, and see what you have missed, what new thoughts occur to you as you look at it again, and make additional notes in the relevant sections, or below.

CHAPTER SIX

EDGE-it In The Moment

*"A wise man can learn more from a foolish question
than a fool can learn from a wise answer."*

– Bruce Lee

Think of a recent time when you had to think on your feet. What
was the outcome? How satisfactory was that?

So it is possible to use EDGE-it to improve your outcomes. We will talk in a moment about what it would look like to apply EDGE-it in the moment and what the benefits would be. In the meantime, how do you know if it would help you?

 Take a moment to complete the following questionnaire:

	Almost never	Sometimes	Often	Almost always
You feel you have your best ideas just after the time when they would be most useful.				
You notice that when you are in pressurised situations you are confused about what is actually happening.				
You find it difficult to narrate what is happening in the moment.				
You are confused by the non-verbal reaction of others in the middle of a conversation.				
You are surprised by the reaction you get to what you have said.				

In the Moment Health Check

Unless all your ticks are in the far left column of answers – 'almost never' – applying EDGE-it in the moment will get you improved outcomes from your Experiences. Applying EDGE-it in the moment will help you build your EDGE muscle and bring immediate improvements. *And it takes virtually no time at all!*

The French have an expression which we met earlier – *'esprit d'escalier'* – 'stairway thinking'. It describes that moment when you leave a meeting, or disconnect from a phone call, or hit 'send' in your emails... and you think of the *perfect* comment to make. EDGE-it in the moment can help you limit these occurrences.

Think of a time when this happened and make some notes here:

So why did this happen? Most likely, it was because you got caught up in the situation, and didn't take a moment to think about what was happening. Perhaps emotions were high. Perhaps it was the stakes that were high. Maybe there was history between you and the other people who were there. Maybe you were on 'auto-pilot'. Or maybe it was simply that you were thinking about the wrong things.

Whatever the reason, in that Experience you had a less than optimal result and you would like it to be different next time.

It is possible for you to use this methodology when you are in an Experience on your own. However, the more difficult context in which to use it is when you are in contact with another person, where the need to maintain rapport is critical to the success of the interaction. Therefore, what I am going to take you through here is just that context – when you are in contact with another. If you are on your own, and want to apply EDGE-it to your in the moment situation, much of what follows will be relevant without any modification.

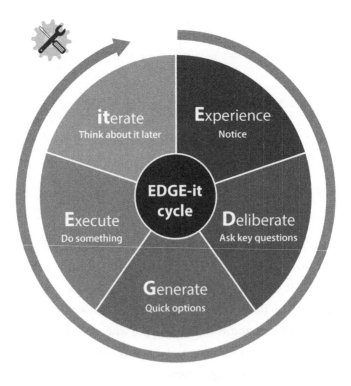

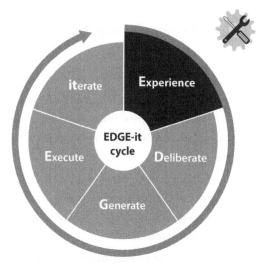

Stage 1 - E – EXPERIENCE

You may remember from the EDGE-it model that this first stage is about Experience. In the last chapter, we focused on gathering facts and feelings about an Experience that occurred in the past. Now I want to think about how you might apply this in the moment, when clearly you will have less time available for reflection.

State

The first thing you need to do is get into the right 'state' for noticing what is actually happening. A state is a concept borrowed from Neuro-Linguistic Programming (NLP) and refers to a kind of energetic 'condition', our mental and physical processes as they exist at any particular point in time. It is kind of like what sort of mood you are in, how you are feeling, what is going on for you inside and out. Examples of states include confident, happy, sad, calm, excited, just to name a few.

Managing your state and your emotions can really help you achieve the outcomes you want in many ways. In the moment, in the Experience you are having *right now*, what state are you in? **This is the first important step: Notice the state you are currently in.**

Then consider what would be the most *useful* state to be in:

- **If you were late to an important meeting with a client because of transport problems, how helpful would it be to get into a calm state of mind before walking into the meeting?**
- **If you were having difficulty convincing a member of your team to change their behaviour, how helpful would it be to get into a positive state of being before continuing the discussion?**
- **If you really wanted to complete a specific project but felt lethargic each time you started to work on it, how helpful would it be to get into an energised state before starting that task?**

What do you think would be the best state to be in to help you notice as much as possible about an Experience you are having? How would you describe that state? Jot down a few words in the box below.

How can you get into that state, though, when you are in the middle of having an Experience? One way of doing it is to set up a 'state anchor' using Neuro-Linguistic Programming (NLP).

State Anchor

Identify clearly the emotional state you want. This step is absolutely crucial. You need to define very specifically how you want to feel. Choosing to feel calm and curious, for example, is specific and something you can work towards using the NLP anchoring technique. Saying that you do not want to feel anxious or tense is not much help because it doesn't state clearly what it is you *do* want.

Now think about a time when you have felt like that before. Recall a specific time in your life when you felt this desired state. Pick a powerful example. It is worthwhile looking back at your memories to relive times when you had this desired state. The context is unimportant. What is important is recalling a few particularly strong experiences and then selecting the most powerful one.

To create the state in your imagination, NLP suggests you should **put yourself back into that experience as if it is happening in this moment.** Notice what you see, hear what you were hearing, feel what you were feeling in the moment. Allow it to be as if it is happening. Notice how the state builds to a peak and then declines.

Now **repeat this process.** This time, just as the state is about to peak, make a unique gesture with the fingers of one hand as you say a word or phrase to evoke the feeling, while also visualising an image that represents the state. For example, clench your left fist as you softly say to yourself *just look...* while you picture someone who represents calm curiosity to you, e.g. a yoga teacher. Hold the state for a few moments, release the physical and mental anchors, and then break the state by thinking about something completely different and changing your physical posture.

Go through this whole procedure about five times to build a resilient NLP anchor. The repetition is crucial.

Test the anchor by 'firing' it – make the gesture, say the word/ phrase in your mind, picture the representative person or place – and check that you do experience the desired state. You will know that you have successfully anchored the state when you can access it by firing any one of the anchors – the gesture, the word/ phrase, the image. You ought to feel the anchored state within 10–15 seconds. If the feeling is not satisfactory, try again with a different experience or using different anchors.

Try it now. See if you can anchor a desired state. Remember it takes practice and repetition to work well.

Another way to access the most helpful state in the middle of having an Experience is simply to STOP for a moment, interrupt the flow of what is happening. This is something you can do by yourself, or possibly by including the other person/ people, if there are others with you in the moment.

What can you do by yourself? You can simply 'intend to attend' to the details of what is happening. Deciding in advance that you will be alert to the details of the Experience, you will notice much more than you would otherwise.

Try it right now. Write down as many descriptors as you can of the Experience you are having right now. When you think you have finished describing it, ask yourself: What else am I aware of? See how much describing you can do.

_____

Change Breath

Another technique that you can use is what is called a 'change breath'. As soon as you become aware that you are no longer noticing the details of what is going on, you breathe out – making a conscious effort to breathe out your assumptions and fixed perspective, and then breathe in – making a conscious effort to breathe in curiosity and calmness, for example, about what is going on.

If it seems appropriate to include others in the process, you can simply ask to 'press the pause button'. You could say, "Let's just stop and think about this for a moment" or "Perhaps it would be helpful to summarise where we have got to so far."

Think about a time in a meeting or conversation when things seem to be moving forward under their own steam, and perhaps running away from you a bit. See if you can recollect the stage when that started to happen, and try to identify something you could have said at that stage that would have changed the situation.

_____

_____

_____

_____

_____

_____

Nehal had the following Experience. She had a team member we will call John, with whom relations were sometimes somewhat strained. As a result of coaching on this issue, Nehal had determined a series of actions to help improve her relationship with John. Part of her strategy was to be sure to engage in some personal conversation with him at least three times a week, as it seemed that he responded well to this closer personal relationship. One morning, Nehal asked John how his weekend had been. She got back a terse answer. Remembering her commitment to engaging in more personal conversation with John, she persevered, asking him follow-up questions about his initial answer. John's replies became shorter and sharper as the 'conversation' continued. A subsequent review of this Experience revealed to Nehal just when the conversation appeared to go off track, and gave her a heightened alertness to an unexpected response from John. The next time she engaged with him in a personal conversation, she was particularly aware of his mood, and when he was again terse, she was able to facilitate John in disclosing a personal issue that was affecting him at work. They were subsequently able to resolve John's difficulty to everyone's satisfaction.

Here Nehal used a 'looking back' reflection to identify something that she could use in the future in an 'in-the-moment' reflection. The point is to work on raising your awareness so that you can notice signals more quickly in the future, enabling you to change course in the moment when that is useful.

Mindfulness

There is much current writing at the moment about mindfulness. This is a general term which essentially means to be in the here and now, noticing what is going on around you. Mindfulness is a useful skill to acquire. Here is an exercise that can help you feel what it is like to be mindful.

Fix yourself one of your regular and preferred drinks. Perhaps this is a cup of tea, or an espresso. Or maybe it is a simple glass of water. Or perhaps if it is a certain time of the day, a smoky single malt.

Sit with your drink in front of you for a moment. Notice the vessel that holds the drink. What does it look like? What does it feel like? Be aware of the colour and smell of the liquid in the vessel. Can you tell what temperature the liquid is? What else are you aware of about the drink itself? Notice how you feel about the drink. What thoughts do you have about the drink? What memories or associations come up for you in relation to the drink? Pick up the vessel. Notice what it feels like in your hand. What happens to your thoughts and feelings about having this drink as you pick up the vessel? What do you notice about your arm as it holds the drink? Get ready to taste your drink. As it gets closer to your mouth, what do you notice about the drink? What happens to the smell and to the colour? What about the temperature? And what happens to *you* as the drink gets closer? What does your mouth feel like? Allow yourself to taste your drink. What does it taste like? How does that compare with what you were expecting? How do you drink it? Do you hold it in your mouth, or swallow quickly? Or something else? Do you sip? Or gulp? What thoughts do you have while you are doing this? What feelings? What body sensations?

This may seem a strange exercise to do. After all, why do you need to know these things about your drink? Of course it isn't that you need to know these things about your drink. More to the point is that exercising your brain in this way, practising to be mindful, changes the structure of your brain permanently. This helps you to be more mindful, more easily, in situations where it really does matter to you to know more about the current situation you are in.

How did that Experience compare with your usual Experience of having that drink? If you were to apply that sort of mindfulness to a business meeting, what might the advantages be? Take a moment now to list some of them.

_____

_____

_____

_____

That was a relatively slow process I imagine, but this sort of mindfulness doesn't need to take long. If you are not convinced, refer back to the objections discussed in Chapter 3. In fact, it *can't* take long if it is going to be useful to you in the moment. The getting ready for it and the doing it need to happen very quickly. The more you practise, the more agile you become. So you need to practise. There is no substitute.

Now that you are ready to notice, you need to decide what it is you actually want to notice. Whatever it is that is happening in your Experience is likely to be not exactly *what* you anticipated would be happening or *how* it would be happening. You need to become a skilled observer. If you just walked in now, and wanted to describe what was happening, what would you say? Developing this observer skill takes practice. At the simplest level, the question you are trying to answer is: 'What is happening right now?'

You have made space in yourself to stop and notice, using NLP anchors or change breath or mindfulness techniques, and now you need to answer that question: 'What is happening right now?'

Justine's Story

BACKGROUND

Justine had been tasked with preparing a series of announcements to support a global launch of a new product. Though the deadline was still three weeks away, she had become aware that conflicting priorities meant that she was going to miss the deadline. Justine had scheduled a meeting with her manager to let him know that this was the case, and present a plan for a rescheduled launch.

EXPERIENCE:

E

▶ Get ready to notice

▶ Notice the Experience

▶ By the end, have a good awareness of the actual Experience

Justine knew that this was an important meeting. In preparation for the meeting she carefully reviewed the important aspects of the situation: the context of the launch, her rationale for planning to miss the deadline, the likely reaction of her manager and others to the delay, for example.

In preparing for the Experience, Justine also considered how she would like to be during the meeting. She decided that she wanted to be confident about her decision making, open to other possible solutions, and calm. She made sure she had five clear minutes before the meeting to go over her notes, gather her thoughts, and settle herself into this desired state.

Justine went to the meeting. As she and her manager got into the discussion about the launch and her decision to miss the original deadline, her manager appeared to be supportive of her decision and proposed course of action. She noticed a sense of relief that this was the case. By bringing her attention to her almost overwhelming sense of relief, she noticed that she was anxious to bring the meeting to a close. This desire to close the meeting seemed to be shared by her manager. Perhaps the meeting was finished?

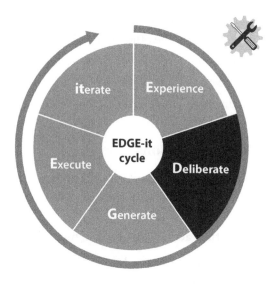

Stage 2 – D – DELIBERATE

Once you are clear what the Experience actually is, you are ready to move to Deliberate. In this stage you are going to make meaning of what you noticed when you were in the Experience stage.

Obviously as you are doing this Deliberating in the moment, it needs to be quick.

Find the focus

The key question in this stage is: **What is the most important thing to focus on right now?** This is something you might work out for yourself. Alternatively, you might want to check with others who are present, asking them: "Where do you think we are right now?" or "How do you feel about what we are doing/about what is happening right now?" Asking others those questions has two benefits: one is that while they are formulating their answer it gives you some time to think; the other is that what they say will help inform you and your thoughts.

The biggest challenges in this stage of the EDGE-it process are to maintain rapport with the other and maintain the momentum of the conversation at the same time as you are trying to Deliberate. The key to success here is to have a clear focus for your Deliberating in the moment.

Two Deliberate Questions

Put the following two questions into your toolkit:

- What is it they actually want from me right now?
- What impact do I want to have with my next action?

The special challenge

It may also be useful to consider options for learning, but only if you are able to maintain rapport and momentum at the same time. If you can, these questions will help you:

- What, if anything, do I want to remember to think about later?
- How will I remember to do that?

The more *prepared* you are to ask yourself these questions, the more likely you are to be able to do it. Going into situations armed with these questions near the front of your mind will undoubtedly help you utilise them. Remember what you worked on in Chapter 1 in relation to establishing habits? This is exactly what you are trying to do here.

DELIBERATE:
D

▶ **Understand the meaning**

▶ **Coax out hidden aspects of the Experience**

▶ **Ask questions**

▶ **What learning do you want to capture?**

Because Justine had thought about how she wanted to be during the meeting, and made sure she had time to prepare for the meeting, she was able to make a deliberate decision to Deliberate on her Experience while the meeting was still in progress. Justine therefore decided to take stock, and ask herself a couple of key questions:

What was the possible meaning behind her (and her manager's) apparent anxiety to close the meeting?

What did her manager want from closing the meeting?

What impact did she herself want to have on the next stage of the meeting?

By thinking (quickly) about these three questions, Justine realised that:

1. She wasn't sure what the meaning was, other than to wonder whether it was related to some sort of underlying anxiety;

2. She wondered if there was some aspect of the implications of this delay that her manager didn't want to shoulder himself; and

3. She wanted to be sure that there were no significant aspects left unconsidered at the end of the meeting.

Justine's Story

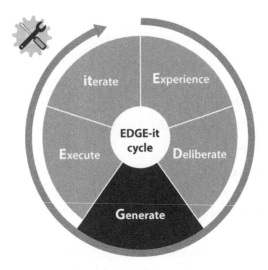

Stage 3 – G – GENERATE

You may not have much time at all for this.

So the challenge is: how can you do this quickly? You have noticed something in the Experience stage, deepened your awareness of it through Deliberate, and now you want to Generate some options.

This is the stage of the process where you are going to Generate two things: the first is the options for action – you need these now; the second is naming the range of opportunities for learning, which can probably wait until after the Experience. Remember that you are not choosing yet, merely Generating.

Prompt questions

It will be useful to have a few favourite prompt questions at your disposal. I recommend having no more than two for an in the moment EDGE-it. Be sure to remember when Generating options that it is essential to think back to your answer to the questions at Deliberate, especially the answer to 'What impact do I want to have with my next action?'

Generator Questions

Possible prompt questions:

What would my _____ self do?
(insert: e.g. calmest, most competent, most creative)

If I just HAD to decide right now, with no more time to think, what would I do?

_____

_____

What would _____ do?
(insert: e.g. Batman, my mother, my boss, Steve Jobs)

If I didn't have to worry about scarce resources
(e.g. time, money, people), **what would I do?**

_____

_____

If this were a close friend instead of a business colleague, what would I say now?
(If this were a business colleague instead of a close friend, what would I say now?!)

_____

_____

_____

_____

What prompt questions occur to you? What questions do you think would be most useful to have on hand for those in the moment situations?

Inner critic

Beware of your inner critic trying to sabotage your thinking. Your inner critic may already be at work here: 'What has Batman got to do with anything?!' 'But I *do* have to worry about scarce resources!' Prepare an answer for that inner critic. You could try, e.g.: 'These are just OPTIONS. I haven't chosen an action yet.' What answer would you want to give your inner critic?

One specific option you might be able to give yourself is more time to EDGE-it. Ask yourself: How possible is it to take a break from the Experience I am having?

GENERATE:

G

▶ Bridge between learning and action
▶ Generous list of options of what you might do
▶ Ask: What could I do?

The most important insight that Justine had as a result of the questions she asked at Deliberate was the third one: she wanted to be sure that there were no significant aspects left unconsidered at the end of the meeting. So the next task was to Generate a number of options to ensure that this goal was met. She had to decide quickly how these options were to be Generated – would she do it herself in her own mind, or involve her manager?

She knew that time was of the essence, and that she needed to consider her options quickly. Justine had two favourite prompt questions:

1. What would my calmest, most receptive self do right now?

    In this case her answer was:

    to wonder out loud, or ask her manager,
    "what else do we need to consider?"

2. If there were more time, what would I suggest?

    In this case her answer was:

    to say, "Let's meet again next week to pick up any loose ends."

She reminded herself that evaluating the options came at the next point in the process, Execute.

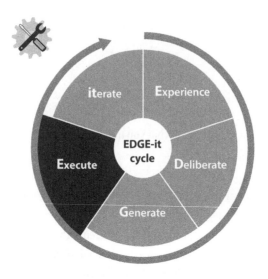

Stage 4 – E – EXECUTE

This is the stage where you quickly evaluate your options and choose the one to Execute. Choose an action and try it out. Consider it an experiment. It will produce a new Experience.

Connect options to outcomes

Key to evaluating your options are the answers you came up with in the Deliberate stage: What do they want from me right now? And: What impact do I want to have with my next action? You want to choose the option that will move you closest to that desired state.

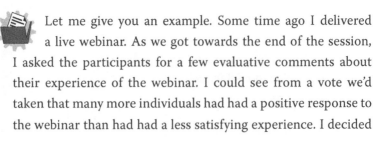 Let me give you an example. Some time ago I delivered a live webinar. As we got towards the end of the session, I asked the participants for a few evaluative comments about their experience of the webinar. I could see from a vote we'd taken that many more individuals had had a positive response to the webinar than had had a less satisfying experience. I decided

to invite three individuals to speak out loud, two positive and one less so. We encountered some technical difficulties that meant the first person invited to speak (a positive one) couldn't broadcast to the entire group. In that moment, I had to reconsider, in a matter of seconds, what it would mean to have only two individuals feed back – one positive and one negative. I considered the two questions:

> **Question 1:**
> *What do they (the webinar audience) want from me right now?*
>
> **Answer 1:**
> *They wanted to know what kind of response others had had to the webinar, and where they individually fitted into that spectrum.*
>
> **Question 2:**
> *What impact do I want to have with my next action?*
>
> **Answer 2:**
> *I wanted to leave the webinar participants with a sense of how successful others had found it.*

I had Generated a few options at that point: open the mic to another individual and hope it worked; open the mic to the two other people I had already selected; or abandon the mic altogether.

Based on the answers I formulated to the two key Deliberate questions, I decided to abandon the mic altogether, say that the mic wasn't working (which it wasn't for the first individual selected), and report the results of the vote instead. It worked a treat for what the individuals wanted from that section, and for the impact I wanted to have.

EXECUTE:

E

▶ Evaluate possibilities

▶ Choose next course of action

▶ End with an action

The first task in this stage is to evaluate the possibilities. Here Justine's challenge was to stay in rapport, think about her answers to the key Deliberate questions, and consider the options she'd come up with in the Generate stage. Fortunately, she'd prepared well for the Experience, and was feeling confident, open and calm.

Justine then combined her main insight from the Deliberate stage – she wanted to be sure that there were no significant aspects left unconsidered at the end of the meeting – with her answers to her favourite prompt questions in the Generate stage – that she could wonder out loud, or ask her manager, "what else do we need to consider?" This gave her an action that she was comfortable to Execute.

So she did just that: she asked her manager,
"What else do we need to consider?"

In response to that question, Justine and her manager began to explore the question of what communications needed to follow, and to whom, and it became clear that it would be advisable to inform the global CEO as soon as possible. That was a good save – obvious perhaps, on reflection, and yet it was nearly lost in the moment of relief that the deadline could be shifted.

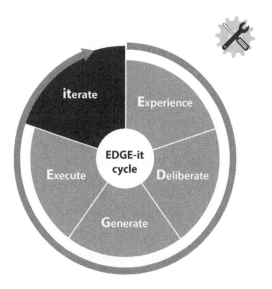

And then finally we come to Stage 5 – -it – iterate

Remember that this just means to go around again. The action you have chosen to Execute has produced a new Experience. Remember the most beneficial state to be in? Notice the Experience you are having. Deliberate on that for a moment. Are you back in rapport, back on track? Or does another adjustment need to be made? Then Generate a new set of options for additional action if necessary. When you've done that, evaluate your options and choose one to Execute. And around you go again.

One of the possibilities for this stage is that there is nothing to stop you from EDGE-ing the in the moment Experience later, i.e., after the fact. Although this sounds rather convoluted, it may well be that the Experience is rich with deeper meaning and further learning, and you could therefore benefit hugely from applying EDGE-it more slowly, and after the fact.

Here is an example. Craig is a training manager for a major operating company in the UK. He delivers training courses many times a week. One day, when he was delivering a course, he noticed that one table of participants seemed less engaged in the training than the others. Applying EDGE-it:

EXPERIENCE: he noticed that the people at this one table were less engaged than those at the other four tables.

DELIBERATE: he focused on the two prompt questions:

> **Question 1:**
> *What do they want from me right now?*
>
> **Answer 1:**
> *They want me to continue to deliver the training.*
>
> **Question 2:**
> *What impact do I want to have with my next action?*
>
> **Answer 2:**
> *I want the flow to continue, and come across as in control of myself and my material.*

GENERATE: Craig developed a couple of options very quickly:

- **ask someone on that less engaged table directly what is going on**

- **invite participants to move around the room in a deliberate attempt to change the energy**

- **step up the pace of the delivery**

- **move on, and hope the table re-engages**

EXECUTE: Craig considered the options in light of the answers he'd Generated at the Deliberate stage and decided to combine two of the options: stepping up the pace a bit and generally move on, hoping the table would re-engage.

In the iterate stage, Craig considered the feedback from the group in conjunction with his own Experience of the training session. The training had been very successful for most of the participants, though those from the less engaged table rated the course more negatively. He decided that he could extract more learning from this situation, and decided to apply EDGE-it after the fact to his in the moment Experience.

He then spent some time on the Experience, and did indeed extract additional learning from it. He realised that in an effort to move the training on, he had effectively sacrificed an opportunity to re-engage that table of participants more effectively. He identified that taking a two-minute stretch break when he noticed the flagging energy on that one table would have likely changed the energy in the room, as well as given him some additional thinking time. He considered the possibility of having decided to shift the seating positions of some in the room after that two-minute stretch break, and concluded that this might have helped more participants engage in the training. The main learning for Craig was that he would benefit from trusting his perceptions more, and making time to accommodate any changes those perceptions pointed to. Result.

Finally, it is necessary to practise. Find a situation in the next 24 hours in which you can practise EDGE-it in the moment.

- ☼ **What situation are you considering?**
- ☼ **How will you remain alert to opportunities?**

E – EXPERIENCE – what technique(s) will you use to ensure that you are in the most helpful state to notice: What is happening right now?

D – DELIBERATE – remember to Deliberate on the key question: What is the most important thing to focus on right now?

G – GENERATE – what are the two most favourite prompt questions that you will take into the Experience with you?

E – EXECUTE – remember to notice the impact of the option you have chosen

it – ITERATE – take note of how the Experience has changed as a result of the option chosen

Record your own example and learning here:

ITERATE:

-it

▶ gain further insight

▶ reinforce rigour of reflective habits

▶ go around again OR reflect on reflecting

Finally, in the last stage, Justine paused for a cycle of iteration. In this instance, she chose to go around the cycle again very quickly, before the meeting with her manager finished.

The **Experience** was that they had nearly missed an important piece of the puzzle, neglecting some essential communication requirements relating to the decision they'd taken together.

In **Deliberate,** Justine and her manager wondered together for a moment how that had happened, and what they wanted to be sure of before finally closing the meeting. They wanted – unsurprisingly – to be sure they hadn't missed anything else important.

The **Generate** stage then posed a couple of quick questions – again using one of Justine's favourite in-the-moment prompts. What would my calmest, most receptive self do right now? In this case her answer was to ask again, "What else do we need to consider?"

And so that is what they did. In **Execute**, they asked again, "What else do we need to consider?" After a few minutes of additional discussion, they concluded there was nothing else pressing, and that Justine would continue to think about it over the next 48 hours. If anything else emerged from the thinking, she would come back to her manager with it.

KEY POINTS

Preparing to notice is an important part of applying EDGE-it in the moment.

✿

We can learn to change our mental, emotional and physical state at given times to help us achieve better results. It takes practice.

✿

Maintaining rapport while applying EDGE-it in the moment is challenging – and can be done. Practice is essential.

✿

Having some key, pre-prepared questions in your toolkit will help enormously.

✿

Your own points from this chapter:

_____

_____

_____

_____

_____

_____

_____

_____

_____

KEY TOOLS
INTRODUCED IN THIS CHAPTER

In the Moment 'Health Check'

✿

State Anchor

✿

Change Breath

✿

Mindfulness

✿

Two Deliberate Questions

✿

Generator Questions

Workbook pages for applying EDGE-it In the Moment

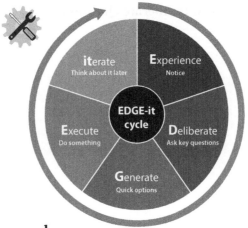

Get prepared

What state do you want to be in for this Experience?

EXPERIENCE

Be ready to return to your preferred state if the Experience turns out to be different from what you were expecting. Practise your NLP state anchor.

Key question: **What is happening right now?**

DELIBERATE

Key question: **What is the most important thing to focus on right now?**

Have the two questions ready:

> **What is it they actually want from me right now?**
>
> **What impact do I want to have with my next action?**

At all times, rise to the challenge of maintaining rapport.

GENERATE

Think about what you *could* do. Include the 'other' in the conversation if possible and appropriate. Take in your two favourite prompt questions, which are:

> **1.**

> **2.**

Remember to consider: **How possible is it to take a break** from the Experience I am having?

EXECUTE

Choose an action and try it out. Consider it an experiment.

ITERATE

Just check: Am I back in rapport, back on track? Or do I need to EDGE again right now, in this moment?

And later

What benefit might there be in applying EDGE-it to this Experience, looking back?

CHAPTER SEVEN

EDGE-it
For the Future

"Rarely do we find men who willingly engage in hard,
solid thinking.
There is an almost universal quest for easy answers
and half-baked solutions.
Nothing pains some people more than having to think."

– Martin Luther King, Jr.

Spending time thinking about what you want can be intensely rewarding or extremely frustrating. Wouldn't it be great if you could spend time thinking about what you want, feeling fairly confident that the time spent will help move you closer to achieving it?

You have decided that you want to learn to apply EDGE-it to something that hasn't happened yet, something aspirational. You have a desired, planned outcome and want to do your best to ensure that it comes to fruition.

Take a few minutes now to think about a goal you have for yourself. Perhaps it is to achieve the next promotion, or win a new piece of work. Maybe it is to resolve an ongoing conflict with a team member, or leave work earlier one day a week. Jot down one of your goals in the box below.

Now let's apply EDGE-it to the goal you have identified.

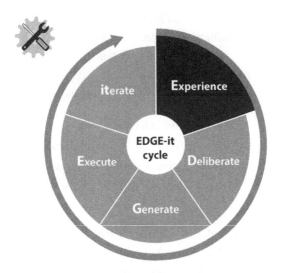

Stage 1 – E – EXPERIENCE

Imagine what it will be like when you have achieved your goal. Put as much detail into the imagined Experience as you can. 'Stand in the future' to describe the goal in what I call 'future perfect' language. That means, describe the future situation *as if it were happening now.*

Here are some examples to help you.

EXAMPLES:

- It has been three months since I set this goal. I have just won a new piece of work from a new client. The work is worth 10% of my annual revenues. I work well within the team servicing this client, and we have built good relationships with two key people at this new client. I speak to my main contact at least once a week, and he rings me at least once a month to ask my opinion about something relating to his business.

- It has been four weeks since I set this goal. I have built the database of marketing contacts I need. All the contacts on there are live, and up-to-date. My PA and I can both access the database easily, and when we have contact with one of the people in the database we update the records.

- It has been six months since I set this goal. I spend at least two hours a week catching up on my reading. In my diary, I earmark one two-hour session a week to leave free of scheduled appointments, and this reading time is sacrosanct. My PA and the rest of my team know that I cannot be interrupted during this time, and I am up-to-date with my technical reading. I have time to think about what I am reading and it is beginning to make a difference to the quality of my strategic thinking. I feel energised by the new thinking I am doing as a result of this reading.

Refer back to the goal you identified at the beginning of this chapter. You are now going to describe the Experience of *having achieved* this goal. Use these prompts to help you. Some of them may not be applicable to your specific goal – if that is the case, just move on to the next one.

 It is now some time in the future and you have achieved the goal you set for yourself.

- How long has it been since you set this goal?

- Where are you?

- What do people notice that tells them you have achieved your goal?

- Who is around you?

- What are you doing?

- How do you feel?

- What do you look like?

- How is that different from how you looked when you set the goal?

- What new behaviours do you exhibit?

- What old behaviours are missing?

- What benefits are accruing to you from achieving this goal?

Describe here your first-draft goal. Describe it here in the way that you will be talking about it *when it has been achieved.* That is, remember to describe it in 'future perfect' language:

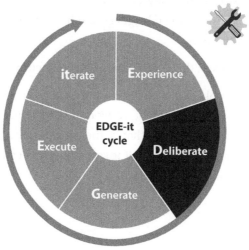

Stage 2 – D – DELIBERATE

Have a look at the first-draft goal you have set. How much detail were you able to describe? If it was very difficult to define many of the details that will be in place when the goal is achieved, perhaps this is a broad strategic goal. If, on the other hand, the details come relatively easily, it is more likely to be a tactical goal.

The danger of leaving your goal as a broad strategic goal is that it may fail due to having too many unknowns to manage on the road to getting there. A strategic goal is never achievable in a short period of time. Examples would include: gaining promotion to a position more than two levels up from your current position in your organisation; expanding your customer base by 20% or more; increasing your revenues by 20% or more, just to name a few. However, each of these strategic goals will have tactical goals (sometimes called milestones) that can indeed be identified. If the first goal you articulated turns out to be more of a strategic goal, it is important to define a number of tactical goals that will be achieved along the way. These are the goals you can work with more easily, as they lend themselves to being described in 'future perfect' language and have fewer uncertainties on the way to them.

For our purposes, this is where you need to focus your attention.

Take a look back at the first-draft goal you set yourself. If it needs any adjustment, re-work it here. Remember to use 'future perfect' language – that is, the present tense, as if it were happening now. Be sure that it is something you can describe in a significant amount of detail.

An example would be:

It has been six months since I set this goal. I have a terrific, mutually respectful relationship with my boss. He includes me at an early stage in many important discussions and decisions. The feedback he gives me in our weekly one-to-ones is focused on the strengths I am displaying and how I can leverage them more fully, with the occasional inclusion of something that isn't going quite so well. I feel confident that I am doing my job well and that he will not initiate any unwelcome 'surprises' in relation to my career prospects.

Or perhaps:

I am now living in my new flat, which makes commuting to the office much easier than it was. In the time I save from the reduced commuting time, I am managing to run for 30 minutes at least four times a week, sometimes five. I have made some financial sacrifices to accomplish this, and am eating out less frequently than I did, but I also have more time for shopping and cooking, and I find I am enjoying that while also making some financial savings.

Your rewritten goal:

It is also important now to think about, to Deliberate on, exactly what the current situation is. You want to identify the various factors that already exist which are supporting the current position, and what could help you achieve your goal, and also what is holding you back from achieving the goal you have set. One useful tool for this is force field analysis.

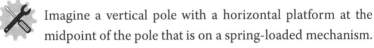 Imagine a vertical pole with a horizontal platform at the midpoint of the pole that is on a spring-loaded mechanism. The horizontal platform represents where you are now in relation to achieving your stated goal. The top of the vertical pole represents achievement of your goal.

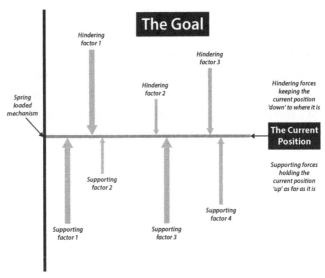

Force Field Analysis

There are a number of factors supporting the horizontal platform from underneath. These are factors that have helped you get as far as you *have* got, keeping the horizontal platform from falling to the ground. These supporting factors can be represented by arrows of different lengths and thicknesses. The heavier/longer/ thicker the arrow, the bigger the significance of that factor.

At the same time, there are some forces exerting downward pressure on the platform. These are the factors that are currently keeping you *away from* the achievement of your goal. These various hindering factors can also be represented by arrows of different lengths and thicknesses. Again, the heavier/longer/ thicker the arrow, the bigger the significance of that factor.

The shorter and lighter the arrow, the less significant the factor. The longer and heavier the arrow, the *more* significant the factor. In this example, you can see that supporting factors 1 and 3 and hindering factor 1 are the most significant in relation to moving *this* current position to *this* specific goal.

Spend some time thinking about what is likely to help you achieve your goal, and what is likely to get in the way. Use the diagram below to help you visualise.

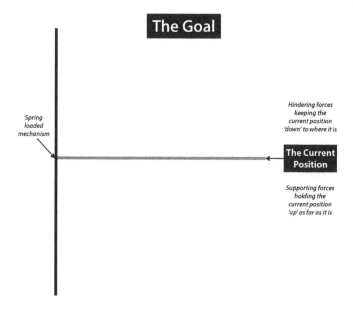

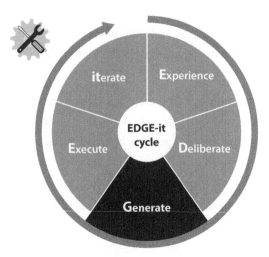

Stage 3 – G – GENERATE

Once you have identified the various factors that are likely to help or hinder the achievement of your goal, it is time to Generate some options. Remember that at this stage you are merely Generating options, the evaluation and choice of specific action comes later. What you are looking for here are ways to achieve your goal.

 Using the force field analysis you prepared, you can Generate three possible categories of options:

- ⚙ **Those that enhance or build on current supporting factors.** These are actions that would at least help to continue to keep the horizontal platform as high up the vertical pole as it is – or even better, push it further up the pole.

- ⚙ **Those that add new supporting factors.** Anything you can add in support of the horizontal platform will push it further up the vertical pole.

- ⚙ **Those that mitigate or remove current hindering factors.** This includes all those actions you could take that would remove the pressures currently hindering the achievement of your goal.

It will be important to explore all three of these categories of option.

Consider:

- ☼ **What has worked for you in the past in situations like this?**
- ☼ **What if you were advising a friend?**
- ☼ **What would make the biggest impact?**
- ☼ **What would you do if you had a magic wand?**
- ☼ **What else could you do?**

When you run out of ideas, ask yourself one more time: What else could I do?

Make your own notes here based on the goal you have selected and the force field analysis you have Generated.

Enhance or build on current supporting factors	
New supporting factors	
Mitigate or remove current hindering factors	

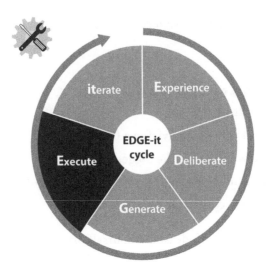

Stage 4 – E – EXECUTE

It is essential to evaluate the options in this stage and choose your actions to Execute. At this stage you should already have a range of options to choose from, and the challenge now is to evaluate them and make your choice(s).

You could use the ease/impact matrix *(opposite)* we outlined when looking at EDGE-it in the past. Another way you could evaluate options is to choose different criteria. Implied in the ease/impact matrix is an assumption that the two key criteria are ease of implementation and impact of the action. What if you chose different criteria: for example, cost and speed of delivery, or impact and cost, or visual appeal and popularity?

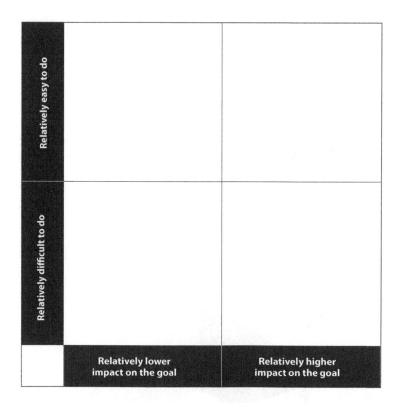

Always, if you are not happy with the choices the tool produces for you, it means that you have not used the right criteria or weighting, or missed something out that actually matters quite a lot to you. Look again. Trust your intuition in this. Consider waiting a day or two and redoing the exercise.

Again, you need to test your commitment to the option(s) chosen. You can use the 1–10 scale that we used in Chapter 5.

Remember to identify the first step, and know *when* you are going to take that step and record it on the next page.

My first step is . . .

And when?

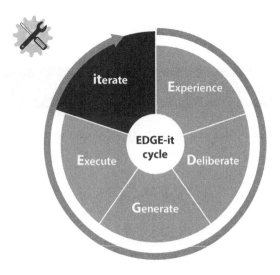

iterate

Experience

EDGE-it
cycle

Execute

Deliberate

Generate

Stage 5 – -it – ITERATE

This is an especially important element of EDGE-it when applied to future goals. During the time you are moving towards the achievement of your goal it will be essential to repeat the EDGE process, checking that the goal is still what you want, checking that the goal is still appropriate in your changing context/ environment, checking that the supporting and hindering factors are still as you evaluated them last time, checking that the actions you are taking are still moving you closer to achieving that goal.

Be sure to schedule in periodic reviews where you can go through the EDGE stages again. Depending on the time frame you have established for achieving your goal, choose an appropriate interval for the next review.

When will you iterate the EDGE process for the goal you have chosen? Make a note here and be sure to include it in any diary system you are currently using.

KEY POINTS

Describe your goals as if you are already standing in
the future. This helps the brain get ready for
the actual achievement.

✿

It is important to be able to articulate your goal with
enough details. If the goal is too strategic, there will be
too many unknowns between here and there.

✿

An analysis of the gap between where you are and
where you want to be (your goal) will reveal factors that
will help you get there, as well as those likely
to get in your way.

✿

Options can include those that:
enhance or build on current supporting factors
add new supporting factors
mitigate or remove current hindering factors

✿

 Your own points from this chapter:

_____

_____

_____

_____

_____

KEY TOOL
INTRODUCED IN THIS CHAPTER

Force Field Analysis

Workbook pages for applying
EDGE-it In the Future

Here you have an opportunity to think of something you'd like to achieve.

EXPERIENCE

Visualise in explicit detail what you'd like to Experience.

In the future time zone, this Experience consists of your goal, described in the language of 'standing in the future' (present tense, as if it is happening now):

DELIBERATE

Create a force field analysis, where the horizontal bar represents where you are now, and the goal you have set for yourself is at the top. Draw on the supporting and hindering forces, using arrows of appropriate length and weight. The shorter and lighter the arrow, the less significant the factor. The longer and heavier the arrow, the *more* significant the factor.

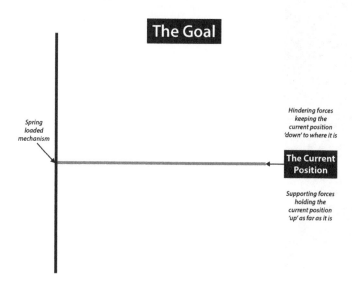

GENERATE

Think of as many options as you can to move that horizontal bar up to the top of your page. When you are done, ask yourself: What else?

Annotate your FFA above.

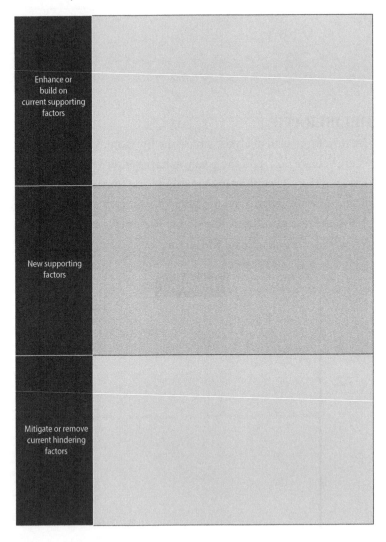

Enhance or build on current supporting factors

New supporting factors

Mitigate or remove current hindering factors

EXECUTE

Use the ease/impact matrix to sort and evaluate the options.

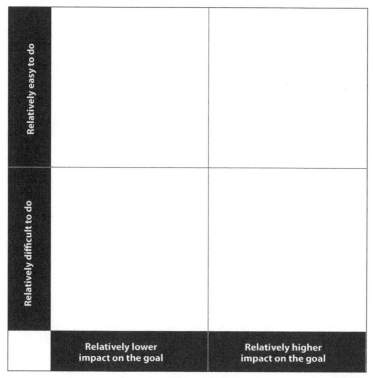

Then choose the one(s) that are right for you. *Be sure to have a first step identified.* Use a scale of 1–10 to test your commitment. If it is less than 10, rethink the action. Keep going until your commitment is at level 10.

Remember to identify the first step, and know *when* you are going to take that step on the next page.

ITERATE

Schedule specific times to repeat the process on your way to the achievement of the goal. **Put them in your diary.**

PART 4

Taking it Forward

*"A reflection in a mirror is an exact
replica of what is in front of it.
Reflection in professional practice,
however, gives back not what is,
but what might be, an improvement
on the original."*

– John Biggs

Better Thinking for Better Results

CHAPTER EIGHT

An Essential Leadership Skill

"Thinking is the hardest work there is,
which is probably the reason why so few engage in it."

– Henry Ford

Now you have seen how EDGE-it can be applied to virtually *any* **Experience: one that has already happened, one that is happening right now, or one that is yet to happen. Hopefully you have already identified the benefits you personally can achieve by applying EDGE-it. Before we finish, let's look at the broader business case for reflective thinking.**

Deliberate thinking, reflecting on what you have done, what you are doing, what you want to do, is an essential leadership skill that you cannot afford to be without. It underpins virtually every one of the tasks you have to do. Thinking is today's main business task, particularly if you are at middle management level or above.

Critical thinking

In recent months and years, books, articles and blogs about a kind of thinking called 'critical thinking' have started to appear. Critical thinking means different things to different people, and if you look for a definition online you will find many complicatedly worded, long-winded, pretty indecipherable definitions. Suffice it to say, for our purposes, critical thinking means applying your thinking to an Experience in an organised and structured way, so that you can understand more than the most obvious layer of it, in order to act with clarity, excellence and precision. In other words, focused, reflective thinking.

Why is there this relatively new emphasis on critical thinking? The demands of the workplace are changing. There is more and more focus on knowledge management and on thinking.

Years ago, it used to be that the main focus of work was physical labour, which of course it still is in some lesser developed parts of the world. Then, with the widespread introduction of electricity and the development of sophisticated machines, mechanised processes largely replaced the physical labour of individual workers. Since the latter part of the 20th century, these mechanised processes have in turn been replaced by computerisation and outsourcing to the lowest cost labour markets. Now that 'knowledge' is fairly universally available, the competitive advantage will come from *using* that knowledge better than anyone else. Always ahead of his time in his thinking about developments in business management, the sage Peter Drucker wrote in an essay in *Atlantic Monthly* in 1994, '...how well an individual, an organization, an industry, a country, does in acquiring and *applying* knowledge [emphasis added] will become the key competitive factor.'

Some well-known business leaders clearly value thinking. Bill Gates, for example, is well known for his 'thinking weeks'. In 2005, the *Wall Street Journal* published an article called 'In Secret Hideaway, Bill Gates Ponders Microsoft's Future.' In the article they revealed that Bill Gates was spending two one-week periods a year essentially in seclusion, reading papers, reading and responding to employee suggestions, and thinking. Although the format of this time away has apparently evolved over the years, the concept remained stable. Bill Gates, one of the most successful businessmen in history, makes regular time to think.

Another successful businessman who actively engages in thinking and encourages others to do so is John Donahoe, CEO and President at eBay Inc. In a posting in July 2013 Donahoe wrote:

'One of the most under-discussed elements of effective leadership is how fast a leader must learn to stay at peak performance. Most successful leaders never stop learning. In fact, they are voracious learners who are always trying to find ways to improve and enhance their own performance and that of those around them.

'I have found that one of the simplest tools for learning and enhancing my performance is to regularly reflect on how to spend my time. Every six months I go through a process where I step back, contemplate what I have learned over the previous six months, and then adjust my focus to ensure I am spending my time and energy in ways where I can create the greatest impact.'

So if these successful business leaders are taking time to reflect and to think, why aren't more people doing it? Why aren't *you* doing it?

Focus on action

I imagine that one reason leaders and people in some organisations (you?) are sceptical about making time for thinking is there has necessarily and appropriately been an emphasis on *action* over the past few decades. Indeed, you are being asked to produce more, with fewer resources, and in less time and for more return on investment (ROI) than ever before. There is a fear that a focus on thinking means taking the focus off action.

On the contrary! It is precisely the act of reflecting, of doing good thinking that will enable you to take the right actions. Efforts to increase productivity have rightly meant a focus on taking action. But people don't always think clearly about which actions to take, and that can lead to bad decisions.

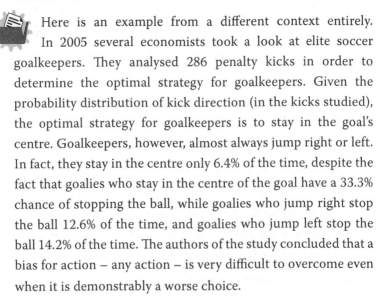 Here is an example from a different context entirely. In 2005 several economists took a look at elite soccer goalkeepers. They analysed 286 penalty kicks in order to determine the optimal strategy for goalkeepers. Given the probability distribution of kick direction (in the kicks studied), the optimal strategy for goalkeepers is to stay in the goal's centre. Goalkeepers, however, almost always jump right or left. In fact, they stay in the centre only 6.4% of the time, despite the fact that goalies who stay in the centre of the goal have a 33.3% chance of stopping the ball, while goalies who jump right stop the ball 12.6% of the time, and goalies who jump left stop the ball 14.2% of the time. The authors of the study concluded that a bias for action – any action – is very difficult to overcome even when it is demonstrably a worse choice.

('Action bias among elite soccer goalkeepers: The case of penalty kicks', by Michael Bar-Eli and Ofer H. Azar and Ilana Ritov and Yael Keidar-Levin and Galit Schein, Ben-Gurion University of the Negev and The Hebrew University of Jerusalem, 2005.)

What is important to notice in this story – though this is not why the economists undertook the study – is that choosing to stay in the centre of the goal is also an action. Choosing to stay in the centre of the goal is the action that will have the best outcome. What is the learning you take from this story?

Deciding to reflect *is* taking an action. Reflecting on which actions to take is a crucial process and key to improving your success rate.

Make your thinking count

Doing things the same way and expecting different results is one definition of insanity. You need to do things differently if you want to improve your results. There is a noticeable and increased emphasis on improved ROI in many organisations these days *in relation to things that have never been measured before.* In my line of work I notice that increasingly organisations are demanding a way to measure the benefit obtained from coaching investment, for example. It is no longer sufficient, if it ever was, to do things 'just because they feel good'. It isn't hard to imagine extending this demand to increased emphasis on returns to be obtained from *thinking*.

One way to ensure that you improve your results is to learn from what you are doing. It makes sense, both commercially and from a personal benefit perspective. Improved thinking brings improved ROI. How could it not? And applying EDGE-it to your thinking gives you the structure you need to ensure that you maximise your investment in the very act of thinking.

So the imperative is clear; you must be better than ever before at acquiring and applying knowledge, at thinking. How can you do that?

Leadership domains

Let's take a minute to look at your role. Consider what you are being asked to do in your role at the moment. Let's decide that the functions for which you have responsibility can be split into four different categories, or 'domains'. We can call these four domains:

- Leading
- Doing
- Managing
- Developing Others

To help you, here is a table already populated with types of tasks. Use these bullet points as prompts to help you think through your responsibilities.

Leading	Managing	Doing	Developing others
• Inspires	• Controls	• Does	• Facilitates
• Motivates	• Organises	• Produces	• Develops
• Initiates change	• Delegates	• Delivers results	• Makes change safe
• Challenges the status quo	• Plans for change	• Accepts change	• Balances challenge and support
• Creates	• Implements current practice	• Accepts current practice	• Focusses on learning
• Sets the pace	• Instructs and directs	• Learns	
• Drives		• Acts	• Balances innovation and procedure
• Inspires loyalty	• Devises procedures	• Follows procedures	
	• Supervises and coordinates	• Administers	• Encourages
	• Seeks productivity	• Seeks own output	• Seeks performance from others
Vision and Future	**Productivity and Results**		**Performance and Learning**
	(Others)	**(Self)**	

Leadership Domains

Take some time to think now about what responsibilities you have, and then populate the following table by placing each responsibility in one of the four columns. Perhaps the columns will not be equally populated. That's fine. It may well be that the amount of time you spend in each of the domains is different from the amount of time you spend in the others. We will come back later to the implications of that, and how you might EDGE-it to your advantage.

Leading	Managing	Doing	Developing others
Vision and Future	Productivity and Results		Performance and Learning
	(Others)	(Self)	

Think about the table you have populated opposite with the tasks you have to do. Clearly there are many skills required to fulfil your responsibilities well. You will have been working on these skills all through your career. And those skills are important.

Applying EDGE-it

You can use EDGE-it to help you work better. You have already seen that as you have worked through the exercises in the previous chapters. Some specific ways you could apply EDGE-it to the domains include the following:

- ☼ **You could select a task category from one of the columns and apply EDGE-it to that task category. This will help you improve your performance in an individual task.**

- ☼ **You could select a column and think about the task categories in it – what is there and what is missing. This will help you strengthen overall performance in a specific domain.**

- ☼ **You could look at the domains (columns) in relation to each other. This will help you improve your overall leadership performance.**

Let's take these in turn.

Applying EDGE-it to a specific category of task

Take some time to consider how deliberate thinking could help you with your categories of task. Choose one task category from each column and think about how EDGE-it could help you.

For example, under 'leading' one of the entries is 'creates'. Polly was responsible for creating a new offering for one of her existing clients. This has the feel of the future time zone, so she applied EDGE-it 'for the future'.

EXPERIENCE – Describe the goal in the language of standing in the future.

It has been six months since I set this goal of creating a new offering for an existing client. I have worked with a team of colleagues over this time, and we have created an exciting new offering. We have discussed this offering extensively with the client, and at least three key client stakeholders are enthusiastic about the offering we have created. No more than two key stakeholders are neutral to the idea, and no key stakeholder is negative. The new offering is already generating additional revenue of £x, and the costs of creating this offering have been less than £y.

DELIBERATE – Analyse the goal and the current situation, identifying hindering and supporting forces.

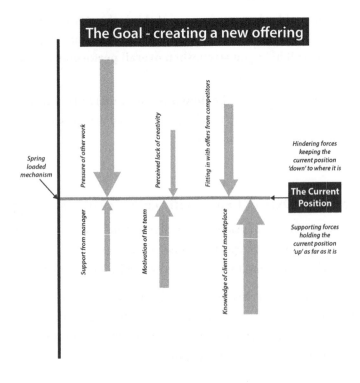

GENERATE – Think of options that could help move the bar of where you are now to the top of the page, where the goal has been achieved.

☼ **Enhancing or building on current supporting factors:**

1. *Get other senior people in the organisation to join the manager in support of the project*

2. *Use the manager's support to get additional resources made available for the project*

3. *Celebrate small successes to build on team motivation*

4. *Attract additional useful people to the motivated team*

5. *Continue to research the marketplace*

6. *Attend trade conferences to build ideas*

7. *Continue to build important relationships with client*

☼ **Adding new supporting factors**

8. *Extend knowledge of existing offerings to other clients by other teams in the business*

9. *Gain clarity about the financial implications of new offerings*

☼ **Mitigating or removing current hindering factors**

10. *Negotiate temporary measures to deal with existing workload*

11. *Include development of new offering as performance objective for the period*

12. *Attend creative problem-solving workshop*

EXECUTE – First, sort the options and choose the right ones for you. Then, be sure to check your commitment to the next step(s).

Using the numbers from the list of options, Polly placed each option into the appropriate quadrant, based on her own assumptions. Continuing this example...

	Relatively lower impact on the goal	Relatively higher impact on the goal
Relatively easy to do	5, 8, 12	3, 4, 6
Relatively difficult to do	11	1, 2, 7, 9, 10

From this analysis, it would appear that options 3, 4 and 6 represented important quick wins. So the next steps could be – taking just one of these for illustrative purposes:

Celebrate small successes to build on team motivation – initiate a weekly celebration to highlight the successes of the week and reward individual or team successes.

When Polly checked her commitment to this using the 1–10 scale, she identified that her commitment to this step was about a 6. That meant it was the wrong step! When asked how this could move up to a 10, Polly identified that rather than a weekly celebration she preferred to have an ad hoc system of celebrations. She established the action of being alert to individual or team successes 'worthy' of celebrating, and to reviewing that at least weekly. Her very first step was to kick off this new 'celebrate success' approach with a celebration of all that had gone before – and planned to have this at the next team meeting. To this action, her level of commitment was 10.

ITERATE – Finally, schedule specific times to repeat the process on the way to the achievement of the goal, and put them in your diary.

Polly scheduled her first repeat for one month's time.

Applying EDGE-it to the task categories in a specific domain – what is there and what is missing?

You could look at one of the domains – let's take the 'doing' domain for example. Again, you could EDGE this from any one of the three time perspectives – looking back on the historic categories that have existed, looking at how it is right now, in the moment, or indeed looking forward to how you would like it to be. It is important to decide where you would like to begin.

The difference is in the **EXPERIENCE** line – what exactly is the Experience you are wanting to EDGE? Here are some starter questions you could use set out under different time zones:

221

Looking back	In the moment	Looking forward
How has it been in the past? Where have you been spending most of your time? What has been missing from this domain? Where have the demands been coming from?	Where are you spending most of your time? What are you neglecting? How is it the same as/different from how it has been in the past?	How would you *like* to be spending time in this domain? What split of activity would feel right to you?
Who are the key stakeholders for this? What do *they* want in this arena?		

Experience Prompts

Some questions may apply across time zones, like the questions about stakeholders.

Also in this stage you will record those thoughts and feelings that you can notice most easily about the Experience. Once you have done this, established the Experience you would like to EDGE-it, you can go on to the remaining stages:

DELIBERATE – making meaning from what you have described. Really dig deep. How do you feel about the Experience you have articulated in the first step? What is the specific learning or outcome you would like to achieve? Spend time being rigorous about the Experience, extracting as much of your thoughts and feelings as you can.

GENERATE – this is where you come up with your possible ways forward. Remember that this is about quantity not quality, so Generate as many options as you can that might help move you forward to the outcome you are looking for.

EXECUTE – now you can evaluate your options and decide what you are actually going to do. Make a plan. Make yourself accountable. Choose the options that will give you the best chance of the best success.

ITERATE – and finally, look back over the process. What have you missed? What else could you include? What new ideas occur to you? What do you notice about the way that you carried out the EDGE process? What would make it even better, this time or next time?

Applying EDGE-it to the domains in relation to each other

You could ask yourself, for example, how much time are you spending in each of the domains? What advantages could there be in shifting the percentages? What is keeping the percentages as they are?

Again, as with the task categories in individual domains, you could use any of the three time zones to describe the Experience:

Looking back	In the moment	Looking forward
How has it been in the past? Where have you been spending most of your time? What has been neglected? Where have the demands been coming from?	Where are you spending most of your time? What are you neglecting? How is it the same as/different from how it has been in the past?	How would you like to be spending your time? What split of activity would feel right to you?
Who are the key stakeholders for this? What do they want in this arena?		

Applying EDGE-it to thinking itself

I want to encourage you to take this even further. What I am suggesting here is that the single activity necessary to underpin the majority of your work as a leader – at whatever level you are in your organisation – is 'thinking'. In particular, thinking more deliberately, in a more focused way – EDGE-ing your thinking – is every bit as important as the other skills you have developed through your career. Go back to the Spectrum of Reflectivity presented in Chapter 1. Thinking is central, and moving from thinking to reflecting increases the likelihood of increasing the time spent doing the 'right' things. Reflecting, which is at the far right side of that Spectrum, adds the most improvement. Reflecting on *thinking* leverages the power of your thinking processes enormously. Peter Honey once said, "Learning to learn is your most important capability since it provides the gateway to everything else you want to develop." I would modify Peter Honey's concept: Reflecting on your thinking is one of your most important tasks. It helps you enhance your problem-solving skills and learn how to apply acquired knowledge in new contexts. Deliberate thinking through applying EDGE-it helps you do just that. It helps you learn from your most important Experiences: those that have already happened, those that are happening right now, and those Experiences you are aiming to have.

The key to this is developing the skill to master the leadership task of *reflecting on your thinking*. This task does not undermine or contradict any of the other important leadership and management skills you have been working on. In fact, it supports them and their development.

Underlying virtually every specific Experience that you want to EDGE is some pattern of thinking, some familiar way of problem solving. Delving into that, developing new insights and skills in how you think and problem solve, will really help you. Thinking about and reflecting on the skill that underlies virtually *all* of the tasks in the table – the skill of thinking – will undoubtedly bring benefits.

What exactly is the 'reflecting on thinking' skill we are talking about? Some of the key elements of good critical thinking are: evaluating assumptions, being objective, using emotional intelligence, considering other perspectives, generating choices, and evaluating alternatives. 'Reflecting on thinking' would include noticing how you do these things, and finding ways to improve the ones that you do less well, and ways to leverage the ones you already do well. This is one of the main functions of the iterate step in the EDGE-it cycle. Here we are thinking about *how* we think, not *what* we are thinking about!

Another way you can use the 'reflecting on thinking' skill is by applying 'thinking' to specific tasks. Let's take the Leading domain as an example. For years you have been told what the key leadership skills are that you need to develop. Your organisation will undoubtedly have an impressive competence framework, or at least a list of the key competencies you must demonstrate in order to advance to the next level. There are training courses and leadership development programmes and mentoring schemes to support you in the development of these key leadership skills. And indeed you have developed many of them, and worked hard in order to do so.

List here some of the key leadership skills that you have developed over the years, together with those you are being told are key to your future advancement:

_____

_____

_____

_____

_____

I would guess that your list of skills includes things such as:

- Create a clear and inspiring vision of the future
- Communicate that vision to your followers
- Motivate others to follow you
- Develop capability in others
- Work collaboratively as part of a team
- Think creatively and innovatively

Am I right?

Well, what all of these skills have in common is that they can all be improved by thinking better, and by extracting more learning from your Experiences.

When I say 'thinking better' I mean using your already well-developed brain (you must have that or you wouldn't already be where you are) in a more focused way. I said at the beginning of this book that reflective thinking is something you already know you 'should' be doing. Over the years you have already got the message that thinking about what you are doing – before, during, and/or after – is a good thing to do. The problem is that until now no one has told you what you need to be thinking *about*!

Two exercises

Let's work through the EDGE-it process in relation to leading.

One way:

Leadership is getting people to follow you. You cannot be a leader without followers. Let's work through the leadership question: 'Why would anyone follow me?'

Take yourself through the EDGE-it process. There are several different ways to do this. You could apply EDGE-it looking back, by identifying an Experience you have already had when people have followed you. Alternatively you could EDGE-it looking back by identifying an Experience you have already had when people have *not* followed you. Another possibility would be to EDGE-it going forward, imagining an Experience in the future when people choose to follow you.

Another way of using EDGE-it in relation to leading:

If you want to 'reflect on your thinking' in relation to a specific task you need to notice more of the details about the way you think.

Choose an Experience of *thinking* to EDGE. Choose a time when you had a decision to make or a problem to solve – key leadership tasks.

Write down here some of the details about that Experience to help put the rest of the process into context:

_____

_____

_____

_____

_____

_____

_____

Now, Deliberate on that Experience. Using the following table, rate your satisfaction with that aspect of your thinking on a scale of 1–10, and answer the prompt questions. The questions given are merely prompts*. Use them in whatever way helps you best. They are not intended to be a checklist, rather prompts for your own thinking. If other questions occur to you, by all means answer them.

* The questions will need to be modified if you are thinking about it in relation to a thinking process taking place at the present time, or in relation to some thinking you want to do in the future.

Critical thinking tasks	Questions to ask yourself (if you are looking *back* on a specific situation*)
Evaluating assumptions 1 2 3 4 5 6 7 8 9 10	What assumptions did I make? On what were those assumptions based? How well did they stand up to scrutiny? What evidence did I have to support those assumptions? What evidence did I have to contradict them? How valid did the assumptions I made turn out to be? How did the assumptions I made affect the thinking I did?
Being objective 1 2 3 4 5 6 7 8 9 10	How objective was I? How objective would others say that I was? What factors coloured my view? How much was my thinking affected by any preconceptions I had? If I was less objective than I would have liked to be, what underlay that? What could have affected my perception of the situation that I was unaware of at the time? How could I have noticed that earlier?
Using emotional intelligence 1 2 3 4 5 6 7 8 9 10	How did I feel at the time? How did others feel? What relationships were important to the decision? How well did I anticipate others' reactions? How well did I manage others' reactions? How well did I manage my own emotional state?

Critical Thinking Assessment

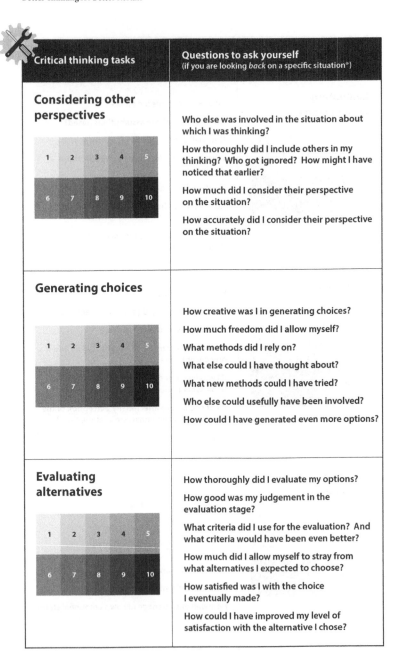

Critical thinking tasks	Questions to ask yourself (if you are looking *back* on a specific situation*)
Considering other perspectives	Who else was involved in the situation about which I was thinking?
	How thoroughly did I include others in my thinking? Who got ignored? How might I have noticed that earlier?
	How much did I consider their perspective on the situation?
	How accurately did I consider their perspective on the situation?
Generating choices	How creative was I in generating choices?
	How much freedom did I allow myself?
	What methods did I rely on?
	What else could I have thought about?
	What new methods could I have tried?
	Who else could usefully have been involved?
	How could I have generated even more options?
Evaluating alternatives	How thoroughly did I evaluate my options?
	How good was my judgement in the evaluation stage?
	What criteria did I use for the evaluation? And what criteria would have been even better?
	How much did I allow myself to stray from what alternatives I expected to choose?
	How satisfied was I with the choice I eventually made?
	How could I have improved my level of satisfaction with the alternative I chose?

Critical Thinking Assessment

Have a good look at your answers to the prompt questions, and any other facets that emerged during your Deliberate stage. What changes do you think might give you the easiest quick wins? What changes might be harder to make, but would also give you a significant positive impact on the facet you want to change? Which aspects achieved the highest satisfaction levels? Which the lowest? Choose one or two elements you want to develop.

The next stage is Generate – what options do you have for improving your thinking? Look at the elements of your thinking that you have chosen to develop. Also look back at your evaluation of 'Generating choices' from the table to see what you might want to consider while you are Generating the new choices. Remember, too, that Generate is about quantity, not quality. Really let yourself go in Generating options for developing your thinking. Keep asking yourself: What could I do? What else?

When you have exhausted the Generate stage of the process, it is time to move to Execute. You can use the 'ease/impact' matrix to help sort these options, or evaluate them another way if you prefer. The most important thing is to choose options to which you feel committed, steps you are actually going to take.

Finally, iterate. Go back around the cycle and see what, if anything, you have missed. Deepen your insights into the area on which you have been reflecting, in order to maximise the benefits.

Improving your own thinking will bring you well-earned rewards I am sure. Let's look briefly now at how improving thinking, and making time for reflecting at an organisational level, can help even more.

KEY POINTS

Deliberate, focused thinking is a key leadership skill that you cannot afford to be without.

✿

Critical thinking means applying your thinking in an organised and structured way in order to act with clarity, precision and excellence.

✿

Focus on thinking does not mean taking the focus off action. Choosing to stand still, like the goalie in our story choosing to stay in the centre, can be the action with the best outcome.

✿

There is increasing pressure to maximise returns on investment in many areas. This can be extended to include the need to make your thinking really count. It makes sense.

✿

Your tasks as a leader in your organisation – at whatever level you are operating – can be categorised into four domains: leading, managing, doing, and developing others.

✿

Applying EDGE-it can help:

- ✿ *improve performance in an individual task in a specific domain*
- ✿ *strengthen overall performance in a specific domain*
- ✿ *improve overall leadership performance*

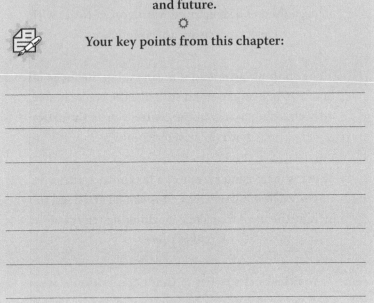

KEY POINTS
(Con'td)

You can apply EDGE-it to thinking itself, to ensure you learn as much as possible from your most important Experiences across all three time zones: past, present and future.

○

Your key points from this chapter:

_____

_____

_____

_____

_____

_____

_____

KEY TOOLS
INTRODUCED IN THIS CHAPTER

Leadership Domains

○

Experience Prompts

○

Critical Thinking Assessment

CHAPTER NINE

Establishing a Reflective Culture in Your Organisation

"Change will not come if we wait for some other person or some other time. We are the ones we have been waiting for. We are the change that we seek."

– Barack Obama

If it is good for individuals to think better, it must also be good for organisations to value good, reflective thinking. In addition to making the change yourself to becoming a more reflective thinker, it would undoubtedly be beneficial to extend that change to your team, your division, your organisation.

Some companies are doing better than others at making sure people have time for reflecting and thinking. Often the purpose of thinking is connected with innovation. Let's look briefly at two examples: Google and Whirlpool.

Google

A number of years ago one well-known benefit of working at Google was established: the '20 percent time' programme. Google allowed its employees to use up to 20 percent of their work week at Google to pursue special projects. That meant for every standard work week, employees could take a full day to work on a project unrelated to their normal workload. Google claimed that many of their products in Google Labs started out as pet projects in the 20 percent time programme. The implication of this policy was that giving people time to think and work on pet projects helped create competitive advantage for Google, both as a benefit to attract the best and the brightest to join Google, as well as in the innovations embedded in the projects themselves.

In August 2013 reports started to emerge from Google head-quarters indicating that the programme was effectively dead. Why would this be? Had Google decided *not* to be innovative? Decidedly not! Rather, Google management took the decision that now a *different* kind of thinking needed to be encouraged in order to promote innovation. Blogs and articles in business magazines and websites proliferate on the question of why Google management took this decision. We don't really know yet, and we certainly don't yet know what effect the decision will have. What is certain, however, is that the decision didn't come without thinking. The implications of the decision remain to be seen.

Whirlpool

Whirlpool's story is somewhat different. At Whirlpool they have focused on innovation through structure, making innovation an integral fact of corporate life in the organisation.

They have systematised innovation as a core competency. On the corporate website it states:

> *Whirlpool Corporation firmly believes innovative thinking comes from everyone, everywhere. Nearly 10 years ago, we launched a worldwide effort to instill innovation as a core competency throughout the entire organization. Since then, Whirlpool employees worldwide have participated in and contributed to innovation-related activities resulting in new ideas, products and services; thus delivering real value to consumers in ways never before seen in either the company or the home appliance industry. Focused on embedding innovation as a core competency, Whirlpool Corporation has made a long-standing investment to build this competency. This investment includes redesigning business processes, training thousands of employees, building an innovation management system and changing the culture of the company.*

Things seem to be changing in many organisations. A number of organisations that don't specifically highlight thinking as a recommended activity appear to be moving towards allowing executives a bit more time to think, perhaps at last recognising that the quality and quantity of thinking time has a direct, positive impact on performance. Coaching programmes, for example, are one way of institutionalising thinking time, at least during the coaching session itself. And if you consider coaching integration in addition to coaching interventions – that is, where coaching is or is becoming part of the culture – then there is clearly a focus on thinking.

Your organisation

Take some time to consider your own organisation. What sort of focus on thinking is there in your organisation? And what could you do to sharpen that focus?

This is, at its core, a culture change project. The challenges of culture change are beyond the scope of this book, though there is much written about them. For our purposes here, however, we can consider this an example of aspirational or future-orientated thinking.

Culture change – EDGE-it

To crystallise your thinking and make the output from that thinking most useable, let's apply EDGE-it. Although it would be possible to apply EDGE-it in any of the three time zones, with regard to culture change the aspirational future time zone is most helpful.

EXPERIENCE – Remember that in the future time zone, the Experience stage of EDGE-it relates to the goal you are setting. Describe here in 'future perfect' language – the language of standing in the future – what it is like when you have achieved the kind of reflective thinking culture you want to have in your organisation. If 'organisation' seems too big, or out of your reach, substitute 'team' or 'division', or other organisational sub-unit. What is it like in this reflective thinking culture? What benefits have been achieved by making the necessary changes? What is happening around you when the organisation is where you want it to be in relation to reflective thinking?

You might want to consider the following list of factors. These are conditions that are likely to support the success of change in the area of deliberate, reflective thinking. Where would you like your team/division/organisation to be in relation to each of these factors? (You will consider where you are *now* in the Deliberate stage of the process as we are using EDGE-it in relation to a future-orientated goal. You could turn this list of success factors into a checklist.)

Success Factors for Culture Change

Key success factors include evidence that:

- The purpose of reflective thinking is clearly linked to the core business strategy
- Thinking has a clear sponsor, and the sponsor is highly thought of in the organisation
- Senior people in the organisation clearly spend time on deliberate thinking
- Leaders are positive role models in encouraging thinking in others
- HR systems are aligned and fully integrated, so that thinking time is specifically rewarded and the outcomes of that thinking are valued
- There is common practice and language around deliberate thinking

When you are satisfied with your first draft goal, move on to the next EDGE-it stage, Deliberate.

DELIBERATE – What is the current Experience you are having in relation to a reflective thinking culture? What is the current culture in your organisation around thinking? What supports whatever degree of reflective culture you have? What gets in the way of extending it? Use force field analysis to draw the situation as it currently exists. Remember that the top of the vertical pole represents the Experience you are aiming to have, your goal, and the horizontal bar represents the current situation. Draw on to your picture the various supporting and hindering factors, making the arrows the appropriate weights and lengths. Think about, for example, what is getting in the way of quality thinking? What is getting in the way of establishing a more reflective thinking culture? What is helping the quality of thinking in your organisation? What supports culture change in your organisation, both specifically in relation to thinking and reflecting, and also in relation to culture change more generally?

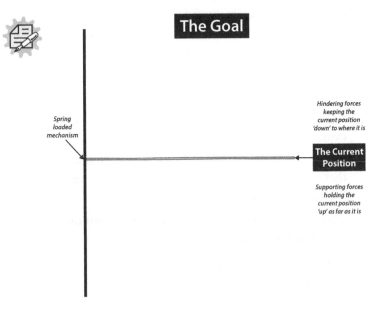

The Goal

Spring loaded mechanism

Hindering forces keeping the current position 'down' to where it is

The Current Position

Supporting forces holding the current position 'up' as far as it is

GENERATE – When you have the force field analysis drawn in a way that most accurately represents the current situation, you can then move on to the options Generating phase. Remember not to censor yourself at this stage, rather to allow yourself free rein. Here quantity is still more important than quality. Generate as many options as you can, in three different categories:

- ☼ **Reduce or remove hindering factors**
- ☼ **Enhance supporting factors**
- ☼ **Add additional supporting factors**

You might want to consider things that you personally can do, as well as things that others could do to help this change happen.

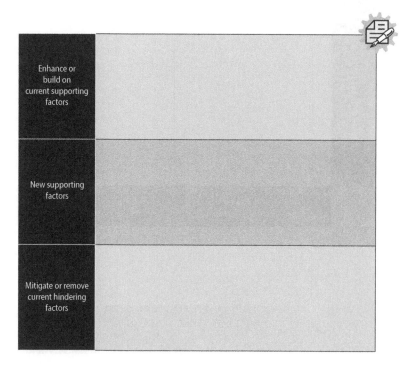

EXECUTE – The next stage is to choose the options from the Generate stage that you think would be good to take forward. Use the tools we have discussed above to help you evaluate your options and choose one or more to Execute. Be sure to test your commitment to the action(s) you choose. It is essential to choose actions that you are actually going to take.

	Relatively lower impact on the goal	Relatively higher impact on the goal
Relatively easy to do		
Relatively difficult to do		

I	2	3	4	5	6	7	8	9	10

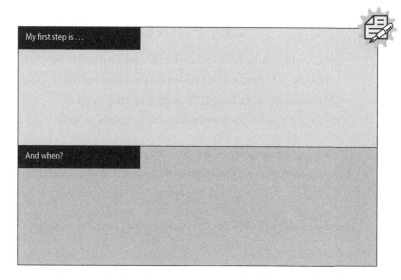

My first step is ...

And when?

ITERATE – Finally, remember to plan in regular reviews. This is the most common application of the iterate phase when using EDGE-it in the future time zone.

KEY POINTS

Some companies have placed a strong emphasis on thinking. This emphasis often has a drive towards innovation at its heart, though the emphasis on thinking can be focused on other benefits as well.

Coaching programmes are one way some companies have demonstrated commitment to institutionalising thinking time.

There are identifiable success factors in creating lasting culture change.

For culture change projects, apply EDGE-it in the future time zone.

 Your key points from this chapter:

_____

_____

_____

_____

_____

KEY TOOL
INTRODUCED IN THIS CHAPTER

Success Factors for Culture Change

Conclusion

As we identified at the very beginning of this book, you already knew you should be doing something to help you improve your results, though perhaps you didn't know quite what that *something* was. I hope that now you can see that deliberate, focused, reflective thinking is a key skill that you cannot afford to be without, and which will help you gain the outcomes you desire.

Focused thinking

Focused thinking brings better results. Focused thinking enables you to act with clarity, precision and excellence. There is an apparent paradox in that spending time doing focused thinking will actually *save* you time, as doing so will help you spend more time doing the 'right' things. Remember the Spectrum of Reflectivity from Chapter 1.

Doing	Thinking	Reflecting
Potential for time wasted in doing the 'wrong' things (decreases as you move to the right)		
	Likelihood of increased time spent doing the 'right' things (increases as you move to the right)	
Performing actions by rote	Asking specific task-related questions	Challenging underlying assumptions
		Investing time in formal process of reflection

EDGE-it

The central model you have learned in this book, EDGE-it, is a five-stage cycle that helps you focus your thinking. The stages are clearly delineated, and straightforward to learn. EDGE-it is a hard-edged, practical model that was designed to be applied in an organisational context.

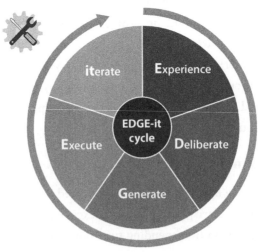

As you have discovered, this model can be applied in any of three time zones: regarding the past, looking back at your most important Experiences; in the moment, to stop that oft-lamented 'Why did I just do that *again*?!'; and for the future, planning ahead to achieve the goals you have set yourself. The basic model is the same in all three time zones, needing only limited time-zone specific adjustments.

Thinking carefully about Experiences you have had and changes you would like to see, applying EDGE-it to the Experiences you *are* having, and *want* to be having, will help move you closer to the results you want. How much closer is up to you, and depends to a great extent on the energy and commitment you give to the process.

What next?

Following this Conclusion chapter, there is an opportunity for you to create your own Afterword. The worksheets there have been included to enable you to apply EDGE-it to your reading of this book. This will help you determine just what is most important for you to leverage from your Experience of reading this book, and guide you towards creating and Executing an action plan to support you in achieving that.

As you will have seen, there are many tools and exercises throughout the book, and you will have spent varying amounts of time and energy on these. Creating your own Afterword will help you identify how best to use *all* the content of this book going forward.

This may include spending more time on exercises you have already done, as well as tackling some that you moved past more quickly. It may include keeping your focus very much on building your own personal habit of reflectivity, as well as shifting your attention to the embedding of more reflectivity into your team or organisation.

You may want to explore in more depth some of the concepts introduced in this book. There is a list of Possible Further Reading included as Appendix 2, and these sources could be a good place to start.

Final words

No doubt by reading this book you have already begun to build this habit of reflective, focused thinking. Keep going! This kind of thinking is a fundamental skill that in today's complex world you cannot afford to be without, an essential habit for success. The more you do it, the more you will ensure that you are spending your time doing the 'right' things and in the best possible way, to help you get the better results you want. Definitely.

Your Afterword

Worksheets for Applying EDGE-it to Your Reading of this Book

So, now that you have read this book, it is time to put the learning into action. Here is a set of worksheets for looking back on your Experience of reading this book, and applying EDGE-it. In order to be able to use these pages as a template for applying EDGE-it to other activities, photocopy the blank pages first.

EXPERIENCE

The objective of this step of the process is to really describe the Experience. It is here that you gather the facts about what happened. At this stage it is not about making meaning, it is purely about gathering the facts. Spend some time recalling as much as you can about the Experience. Fill in the table below with as much as you can recall. When you have finished, ask yourself: What else?

Note: The 'Others' column may not be applicable if you have read the book on your own. However, if you have spent time discussing any of the concepts or activities with others, this column may indeed be useful in describing your Experience.

Gather facts and feelings	Self	Others
See and hear?		
Do?		
Feel?		

DELIBERATE

The objective of this step of the process is to really make meaning from the Experience. Here, you really want to challenge yourself to go deeper into the Experience, broadening and deepening your perspective on it.

Begin anywhere, take the questions in any order, revisit questions. The questions here are merely examples. Remember that the questions themselves are not the process, they are merely stimuli for your thinking. The focus is on the two points in the centre of the circle. Deliberate on your Experience. Go as deep as you can.

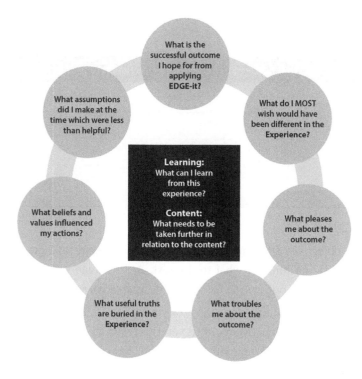

Learning/Content Question Wheel

_____

_____

_____

_____

LEARNING: What can I learn from this Experience?

_____

_____

_____

_____

CONTENT: What needs to be taken further in relation to the content?

_____

_____

_____

_____

GENERATE

The objective of this step of the process is to begin to Generate options – options for what to do next. At this stage you are _not_ evaluating the options, so feel free to be as creative as you can be.

It is important at this stage to allow yourself to Generate as many options as possible. Many of us tend to restrict our thinking to 'either.../or...' thinking, which limits the chance we will find the 'best' options. However many options you Generate, always try to get a few more. Ask yourself: What else?

Options for achieving the objectives determined in Deliberate include:

1 _____	16 _____
2 _____	17 _____
3 _____	18 _____
4 _____	19 _____
5 _____	20 _____
6 _____	21 _____
7 _____	22 _____
8 _____	23 _____
9 _____	24 _____
10 _____	25 _____
11 _____	26 _____
12 _____	27 _____
13 _____	28 _____
14 _____	29 _____
15 _____	30 _____

EXECUTE

The objective of this step of the process is to decide what you are actually going to do. This could be either the next step, or a whole plan, or both. At this stage you need to evaluate your options and test your commitment to them.

You can do this in three steps:

1. **First, take all the options you have Generated and place them into the ease/impact grid. Be sure to consider:**

   What assumptions am I making that lead me to place this option in this quadrant? How do I know these assumptions are right? What else could be true?

   Move the options into different quadrants if necessary.

	Relatively lower impact on the goal	Relatively higher impact on the goal
Relatively easy to do		
Relatively difficult to do		

2. Decide what you are going to do next. You might want to consider the very next step, or, if you have loads of good ideas Generated, you may want the next step to be to make a plan, to incorporate many of the ideas you have Generated.

3. Finally, test your level of commitment to the action. Using a scale of 1 to 10, where 1 is 'I am not going to do this, but I had to come up with something' and 10 is 'I absolutely will do this – I can hardly wait to stop reading this book so I can make it happen', assign a number to your level of will to Execute each option.

1	2	3	4	5	6	7	8	9	10

The actions I commit to doing are:

_____

_____

_____

_____

_____

_____

ITERATE

This is to repeat, to go around again. This step of the EDGE-it cycle is useful for reflecting on the *process* of reflecting itself. Go back over the process you just completed, and apply EDGE-it to that. You could ask, for example:

- ☼ **What do I notice about how I reflected?**
- ☼ **What did I miss?**
- ☼ **What did I focus on?**
- ☼ **What were the difficult parts?**
- ☼ **What was easier?**
- ☼ **Where was I most engaged?**
- ☼ **What would I like to do differently next time?**
- ☼ **How could I make that happen?**
- ☼ **What *will* I do differently next time?**

This stage of EDGE-it is also useful in going back over the content. You could go back over your workings in this section, and see what you have missed, what new thoughts occur to you as you look at it again, and make additional notes in the relevant sections.

APPENDIX I

A Brief History of Reflective Practice, with Models

STAGE ONE – Why Reflection Matters
John Dewey

According to many people, the concept of reflective thinking was first written about by John Dewey, an American philosopher and psychologist active in the field of educational reform in the late 19th and early 20th centuries. He wrote extensively about reflective thinking, and its application for problem solving. According to Dewey, the main purpose of reflective thinking was to make order out of incongruity and dissonance. Key to his thinking was that reflective thinking is called for when people recognise that some problems cannot be solved with certainty. He identified five phases, or aspects, of reflective thought:

1. suggestions, in which the mind leaps forward to a possible solution;

2. an intellectualization (sic) of the difficulty or perplexity that has been felt (directly experienced) into a problem to be solved, a question for which the answer must be sought;

3. the use of one suggestion after another as a leading idea, or hypothesis, to initiate and guide observation and other operations in collection of factual material;

4. the mental elaboration of the idea or supposition (reasoning, in the sense in which reasoning is a part, not the whole, of inference); and

5. testing the hypothesis by overt or imaginative action.

John Dewey, *How We Think*, Lexington, Mass.: DC Heath and Company, 1933, p.107

Donald Schön

Another significant figure in the story of the development of reflective thinking was the American social scientist, consultant and thinker Donald Schön. Working and writing in the second half of the 20th century, one of Schön's seminal works, *The Reflective Practitioner*, was published in 1983. In this important book, Schön wrote about the concepts of 'reflection in action' and 'reflection on action', as experienced by professionals working in five fields: engineering, architecture, management, psychotherapy and town planning. His basic premise was that to be successful professionals need to be able to 'think on their feet', to notice when things are not going as expected, and determine a revised course of action. Although there has been some disagreement in more recent times about Schön's concepts of reflecting in action and reflecting on action, most would agree that his thinking and writing have progressed learning theory. It was no longer 'required' to learn from errors made, rather it was possible to notice *in the moment* that events were unfolding differently than expected, and to stop and take corrective action.

Donald Schön, *The Reflective Practitioner: How Professionals Think In Action*, New York: The Perseus Books Group, 1983

David Kolb

Another important contributor to modern understanding of learning theory and the role of reflection in learning was David Kolb. In the 1970s, working with a colleague Ron Fry, Kolb developed the Experiential Learning Model. This model formally included a reflection stage as a necessary element of effective learning. In 1984, Kolb translated this learning model into Learning Styles and published *Experiential Learning: experience as a source of learning and development.*

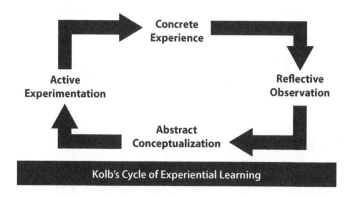

Kolb's Cycle of Experiential Learning

Honey and Mumford

Peter Honey and Alan Mumford developed their learning styles system as a variation on the Kolb model while working on a project for the Chloride corporation in the 1970s. Honey and Mumford say of their system:

"Our description of the stages in the learning cycle originated from the work of David Kolb. Kolb uses different words to describe the stages of the learning cycle and four learning styles... The similarities between his model and ours are greater than the differences."

Peter Honey and Alan Mumford, *The Manual of Learning Styles*, 3rd edition, 1992

Honey and Mumford coined the following terms to describe the four different learning styles:

- ☼ **Activist**
- ☼ **Reflector**
- ☼ **Theorist**
- ☼ **Pragmatist**

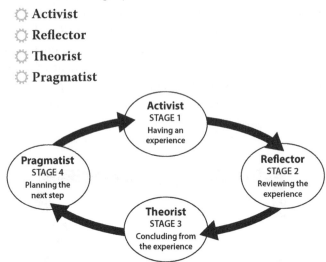

STAGE TWO – How to Reflect

Terry Borton

An American teacher, Terry Borton, writing in a book called *Reach, Touch and Teach* published by McGraw Hill in 1970, identified three key questions to use in increasing self-knowledge, something he described as '...as difficult to obtain as it is powerful' (p.93). He went on to outline the three questions: What? So What? and Now What? Borton wrote: 'The What, So What, Now What model...provides an organised way of increasing awareness (What), evaluating intention (So What), and experimenting with new behaviour (Now What).' (p.93)

Borton's three stem questions were further developed by John Driscoll in 1994, 2000 and 2007, matching the stem questions with stages in Kolb's experiential learning cycle, and adding additional trigger questions. Though the context of Driscoll's extensions to the Borton model was nursing, the general approach is applicable in virtually any reflective context.

Graham Gibbs

Professor Graham Gibbs published his Reflective Cycle in his 1988 book *Learning by Doing*. In section 4.3.5, he states that the diagram he presents 'relates the stages of a full structured debriefing to the stages of the experiential learning cycle'. The diagram looks something like this:

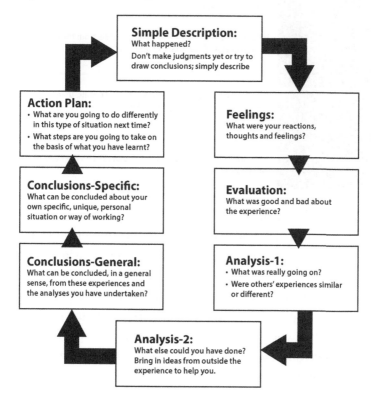

He goes on to elaborate somewhat on the various stages of the cycle as follows:

Description	What happened? Don't make judgements yet or try to draw conclusions; simply describe.
Feelings	What were your reactions and feelings? Again don't move on to analysing these yet.
Evaluation	What was good or bad about the experience? Make value judgements.
Analysis	What sense can you make of the situation? Bring in ideas from outside the experience to help you. What was really going on? Were different people's experiences similar or different in important ways?
Conclusions (general)	What can be concluded, in a general sense, from these experiences and the analyses you have undertaken?
Conclusions (specific)	What can be concluded about your own specific, unique, personal situation or way of working?
Personal action plans	What are you going to do differently in this type of situation next time? What steps are you going to take on the basis of what you have learnt?

Christopher Johns

Christopher Johns' model arose from work in the nursing context in the early 1990s. His intention was initially to help us make explicit the knowledge nurses used in practice. Though this thinking was originally formulated in the context of nursing, it can readily be applied in any reflective context. Johns' first published models used cue questions, divided to promote more detailed reflection. You can see the evidence of the nursing context in a number of the questions:

1. Description of the experience

Phenomenon – describe the here and now experience

Causal – what essential factors contributed to this experience?

Context – what are the significant background factors to this experience?

Clarifying – what are the key processes for reflection in this experience?

2. Reflection

What was I trying to achieve?

Why did I intervene as I did?

What were the consequences of my actions for:

Myself? The patient/family? The people I work with?

How did I feel about this experience when it was happening?

How did the patient feel about it?

How do I know how the patient felt about it?

3. Influencing factors

What internal factors influenced my decision making?

What external factors influenced my decision making?

What sources of knowledge did/should have influenced my decision making?

4. Evaluation:

Could I have dealt with the situation better?

What other choices did I have?

What would be the consequences of these choices?

5. Learning

How do I now feel about this experience?

How have I made sense of this experience in light of past experiences and future practice?

How has this experience changed my ways of knowing?

Empirics – scientific

Ethics – moral knowledge

Personal – self-awareness

Aesthetics – the art of what we do, our own experiences

Johns has continued to be active in thinking and writing about reflective practice, and published a new edition of his book *Becoming a Reflective Practitioner* in 2013. (Wiley-Blackwell)

APPENDIX 2

Possible Further Reading

Cochran, W and **Tesser, A (1996)** 'The "what the hell" effect: some effects of goal proximity and goal framing on performance', Striving and feeling: interactions among goals, affect, and self-regulation, pp. 99–120

Di Stefano, G and **Gino, F** and **Pisano, G** and **Staats, B (March 25, 2014)** 'Learning by Thinking: How Reflection Aids Performance', Harvard Business School NOM Unit Working Paper No. 14-093

Gibbs, G (1988) *Learning by doing: a guide to teaching and learning methods,* Oxford: Oxford Brookes University Further Education Unit

Honey, P and **Mumford, J (1982)** *Manual of Learning Styles,* London: P Honey

Johns, C (2013) *Becoming a Reflective Practitioner (Fourth Edition),* Wiley-Blackwell

Kegan, R and **Lahey, L (2009),** *Immunity to Change: how to overcome it and unlock the potential in yourself and your organization,* Boston, Massachusetts: Harvard Business Press

Kolb, D (1984) *Experiential Learning: experience as the source of learning and development,* Englewood Cliffs, New Jersey, US: Prentice Hall

Moon, JA (2004) *A handbook of reflective and experiential learning: theory and practice,* London: Routledge

Prochaska, J and **DiClemente, C (1983)** 'Stages and processes of self-change in smoking: toward an integrative model of change', *Journal of Consulting and Clinical Psychology,* 5, pp. 390–395

Schön, D (1983) *The Reflective Practitioner: How professionals think in action,* New York, US: Basic Books

About the Author

Cathy Lasher approaches personal and professional development from the perspective of 'if you are going to put the effort in, it really has to make a difference.'

Cathy has been a university lecturer in reflective practice for the last few years. She is also an executive and business coach, and leadership development specialist, working with blue chip corporate clients and professional services firms, as well as public sector and not-for-profit clients. A businesswoman with wide experience over more than 20 years of helping enterprises improve their performance through enhancing the leadership capabilities of individuals, she combines robust academic skills in reflective thinking and formal qualifications as a chartered accountant and an MBA, with formal qualification as a relational psychotherapist and outstanding skills as a coach, facilitator and developer of talent. This combination enables her to offer a pragmatic business edge, underpinned by rigorous academic knowledge and solid psychological grounding.

American by birth, Cathy has been here in the UK for nearly 35 years, though many still ask her: "What time did your plane arrive at Heathrow?" Perhaps she still has a strong American accent!

Testimonials

"As a productivity specialist, whose watch-word is 'leverage,' I am delighted to see reflective practice propelled into the mainstream. Cathy not only makes a powerful business and personal case for the efficacy of focused thinking but she also makes it instantly accessible with a practical toolkit. A must-read for the busy professional in search of better results amid the chaos and complexity of the twenty-first century workplace."

Carol McLachlan, *Head of Leadership, Manchester Airport Group*

"After years of coaching clients for success, I have seen how those who know how to think reflectively develop that all-important edge needed to achieve their goals. To our good fortune, Cathy Lasher's book delivers the how-to of reflective thinking with a clear voice and all the tools you'll ever need."

Dawn Lennon, *author, Business Fitness: The Power to Succeed - Your Way*

"Continuous learning is crucial for any manager's development. Cathy's coaching approach is instrumental in breaking dysfunctional patterns and reinforcing beneficial ones. This book translates her insights into a highly readable and practical guide to self-development."

General Manager, *leading European airline group*

"It is increasingly recognised that focused thinking is an essential leadership skill. No longer are leaders seen to be silver bullet, supermen; a good leader takes time to reflect, to consult with others, to think, plan and learn. Indeed, in her book, Cathy quotes Harvard research (Di Stefano et al 2014) that demonstrates that 'as little as ten minutes of reflection brings significant improvements in learning and doing.'

However, too many of us spent much of our lives being told what to think rather than being taught how to think. We don't know the skills of 'reflective practice.' This book changes all that. With EDGE-it, Cathy takes the reader though a journey of development. Drawing on masses of well-researched material into reflective practice, she has developed an accessible model for busy professionals. The book is packed full of exercises and rich examples that come from Cathy's many years as a consultant, coach and therapist. It is a pleasure to read and a real contribution to leadership skills."

Professor Charlotte Sills, Ashridge Business School and Metanoia Institute, UK

"As a busy executive, I want to know what successful people do, and learn how to do it too. This book is packed with powerful examples and easy-to-do, impactful exercises. You can use it as a one-day self-coaching kit, and dip back into it over time. Learning to apply EDGE-it will really move things forward for you."

Senior business executive

Lightning Source UK Ltd.
Milton Keynes UK
UKOW06f1524120615

253415UK00001B/9/P